Praise for *Real Time Leadership Development*

"This book is a highly accessible, comprehensive compendium of leadership development strategies and a 'must read' for anyone trying to improve his or her own skills or those of another."

Nancy T. Tippins, Senior Vice President and
Managing Principal, Valtera Corporation

"Drs. Yost and Plunkett have achieved a great feat – delivering practical developmental advice that is rooted in research. I highly recommend their book to anyone who wishes to develop stronger leadership skills."

Robert E. Lewis, PhD, Director, APT, Inc.

"Mary Mannion Plunkett and Paul Yost did something remarkable in the exploration of leadership and career development: they asked leaders themselves about development experiences; they did it in a systematic and scientific way; they applied it to a diagonal and diverse slice of company managers; and they tracked careers through a longitudinal study over many years. *Real Time Leadership Development* provides unique insight into seminal career events that produce real learning, provoke actual behavior change, and cause leadership evolution. It also shows real insight into the responsibility of leaders (and the tools they can use) to develop successors.

We should have known this all along; ask a retired executive what she/he remembers of their career and rarely will you hear about a course they took or a book they read. Mostly they will recall the challenges they experienced in their first staff assignment where they had responsibility without authority; the time they presided over a task force to fix something that was broken; the time they gave themselves a failing grade (even if the organization gave them a pass) for lacking the courage to speak truth to power; and so on.

Real Time Leadership Development is more than a distillation of career change pointers from the authors' own research. In it you will also find best practices in traditional tasks of leadership development: performance management, mentoring, networking, leadership training, high potential and succession management, and systematic human resource development.

Kudos to Mary and Paul for shining a spotlight of facts and data on previously mysterious and opinion-laden processes, and on what stimulates authentic evolution of lead[...] [...] of us. And for providing useful, easily [...] in an accessible format to implement [...] human resource and leadership devel[...]

Peter M. Morton, VP Lea[...]
The Boeing Company; VP Human Resources (retired),
Boeing Commercial Airplanes

Talent Management Essentials

Series Editor: Steven G. Rogelberg, Ph.D
Professor and Director Organizational Science, University of North Carolina – Charlotte

Senior Advisory Board:
- Eric Elder, Ph.D., Director, Talent Management, Corning Incorporated
- William H. Macey, Ph.D., Chief Executive Officer, Valtera Corporation
- Cindy McCauley, Ph.D., Senior Fellow, Center for Creative Leadership
- Elaine D. Pulakos, Ph.D., Chief Operating Officer, PDRI, a PreVisor Company
- Douglas H. Reynolds, Ph.D., Vice President, Assessment Technology, Development Dimensions International
- Ann Marie Ryan, Ph.D., Professor, Michigan State University
- Lise Saari, Ph.D., Direct, Global Workforce Research, IBM
- John Scott, Ph.D., Vice President, Applied Psychological Techniques, Inc.
- Dean Stamoulis, Ph.D., Managing Director, Executive Assessment Practice Leader for the Americas, Russell Reynolds Associates

Special Features

Each volume contains a host of actual case studies, sample materials, tips, and cautionary notes. Issues pertaining to globalization, technology, and key executive points are highlighted throughout.

Titles in the Talent Management Essentials series:

Performance Management: A New Approach for Driving Business Results
Elaine D. Pulakos

Designing and Implementing Global Selection Systems
Ann Marie Ryan and Nancy T. Tippins

Designing Workplace Mentoring Programs: An Evidence-Based Approach
Tammy D. Allen, Lisa M. Finkelstein, and Mark L. Poteet

Career Paths: Charting Courses to Success for Organizations and Their Employees
Gary W. Carter, Kevin W. Cook, and David W. Dorsey

Mistreatment in the Workplace: Prevention and Resolution for Managers and Organizations
Julie B. Olson-Buchanan and Wendy R. Boswell

Developing Women Leaders: A Guide for Men and Women Organizations
Anna Marie Valerio

Employee Engagement: Tools for Analysis, Practice, and Competitive Advantage
William H. Macey, Benjamin Schneider, Karen M. Barbera, and Scott A. Young

Online Recruiting and Selection: Innovations in Talent Acquisition
Douglas H. Reynolds and John Weiner

Senior Executive Assessment: A Key to Responsible Corporate Governance
Dean Stamoulis

Real Time Leadership Development
Paul R. Yost and Mary Mannion Plunkett

Real Time Leadership Development

Paul R. Yost and
Mary Mannion Plunkett

WILEY-BLACKWELL

A John Wiley & Sons, Ltd., Publication

This edition first published 2009
© 2009 Paul R. Yost and Mary Mannion Plunkett

Blackwell Publishing was acquired by John Wiley & Sons in February 2007. Blackwell's publishing program has been merged with Wiley's global Scientific, Technical, and Medical business to form Wiley-Blackwell.

Registered Office
John Wiley & Sons Ltd, The Atrium, Southern Gate, Chichester, West Sussex, PO19 8SQ, United Kingdom

Editorial Offices
350 Main Street, Malden, MA 02148-5020, USA
9600 Garsington Road, Oxford, OX4 2DQ, UK
The Atrium, Southern Gate, Chichester, West Sussex, PO19 8SQ, UK

For details of our global editorial offices, for customer services, and for information about how to apply for permission to reuse the copyright material in this book please see our website at www.wiley.com/wiley-blackwell.

The right of Paul R. Yost and Mary Mannion Plunkett to be identified as the author of this work has been asserted in accordance with the Copyright, Designs and Patents Act 1988.

Wiley also publishes its books in a variety of electronic formats. Some content that appears in print may not be available in electronic books.

Designations used by companies to distinguish their products are often claimed as trademarks. All brand names and product names used in this book are trade names, service marks, trademarks or registered trademarks of their respective owners. The publisher is not associated with any product or vendor mentioned in this book. This publication is designed to provide accurate and authoritative information in regard to the subject matter covered. It is sold on the understanding that the publisher is not engaged in rendering professional services. If professional advice or other expert assistance is required, the services of a competent professional should be sought.

Library of Congress Cataloging-in-Publication Data

Yost, Paul R.
   Real time leadership development / Paul R. Yost and Mary Mannion Plunket.
       p. cm. – (Talent management essentials)
   Includes bibliographical references and index.
   ISBN 978-1-4051-8675-9 (hardcover : alk. paper) – ISBN 978-1-4051-8667-4 (pbk. : alk. paper)
   1. Leadership.   2. Executive ability.   I. Plunket, Mary Mannion.   II. Title.

   HD57.7.Y67   2009
   658.4′092–dc22

                                              2008046993

A catalogue record for this book is available from the British Library.

Icon in Case Scenario boxes © Kathy Konkle / istockphoto.com

Set in 10.5 on 12.5 pt Minion by SNP Best-set Typesetter Ltd., Hong Kong
Printed and bound in Singapore by Fabulous Printers Pte Ltd

1   2009

Contents

Foreword

Getting Development Out of the Little Box at the End of a Form

Some years ago I was asked to review 200 development plans generated by high potential managers and their bosses at a Fortune 100 corporation long considered a benchmark for developing executive talent. The development plan was one part of a fairly typical performance appraisal form. The form was two pages in length and started with a list of specific business objectives on which the person was rated from "far exceeded expectations" to "below expectations," followed by a routine list of competencies rated from 1 (low) to 5 (high), then a section for comments. At the bottom of the second page was a box labeled "development plan." My task was simply to read the plans and see if I thought they were effective.

The company, though extremely well regarded for its development of managerial talent, clearly was not living up to its reputation through what was in those little boxes. First of all, most of them were empty. Of those containing an entry, the most frequent plan was a stated intention to do more or less of something (for example, communicate more, be less autocratic) or to attend one of the many courses offered by the company or by an outside vendor. Only occasionally was someone to get a coach, and rarely did anyone mention a job assignment or project as a developmental activity. Not all company development plans are confined to a little box on the last page of the appraisal form, but they often share the characteristics I saw in this sample. They are superficially done, almost exclusively about participating in programs, encompass six months to a year in duration, and are unconnected in any meaningful way to the strategic aims of the business. And – not that it matters for such plans – rarely is anyone held accountable for their implementation or success.

It was over two decades ago now (perish the thought!) that we began at the Center for Creative Leadership to explore how executives developed through experience. That work, which identified 16 types of experience and the lessons they could teach, has been replicated in numerous organizations in the United States and abroad. The accumulated evidence makes a solid case that superficial activities have little developmental impact and that challenging experiences, not programs, should drive the executive development process. Subsequent work has identified what makes experiences powerful, suggested ways that developmental experiences can be linked to the business strategy, and conjectured about how to help people learn from the experiences they have. The resulting conceptual model of development offers an alternative to the vacuous box at the end of the appraisal form, an approach based on the systematic use of experience to develop the leadership talent required to execute the business strategy.

The problem was that it was mostly conceptual. To be sure, pieces and parts had substantial empirical support, but missing was the boldness to apply the ideas in an organization and the patience to develop the tools people needed to make effective use of their experiences. That missing piece is precisely what Paul Yost and Mary Mannion Plunkett have provided in this remarkable book. In their work across several organizations, they not only have identified the experiences that matter and what can be learned from them, they also have developed a framework and the tools needed to put that knowledge to use. They offer a concrete way for individuals to grow and develop at the same time they are running the business.

No one can make someone else grow, and no one cares as much about growth as the person it benefits most. For that reason the authors decided that the best place to start was with people who wanted to develop themselves. But when it came to how to empower individuals to take charge of the process, the authors (despite their knowledge of what the significant experiences are) essentially had to start from scratch. Adding to the challenge, they were trying to get the attention and commitment of busy, pragmatic, action-oriented people who weren't always receptive to the garden-variety human resources fruit salad of offerings. Therein lies the genius: Not only did they generate a strategically relevant, data-based understanding of experiences and the lessons they offer, presented in managerial language, but they were able to develop a set of fun and easy-to-use tools, create a need for those tools, and then make them available.

What you will find in the pages ahead goes a long way toward getting rid of the box at the end of the form. There are questions that will help individuals understand how the business strategy links to development, think through their own sense of purpose and what they hope their legacies to be, and consider the balance they want between work and the rest of life, thus breaking out of the parochial and ineffective year-at-a-time perspective on development. There are other exercises that guide self-assessment and diagnosis not only of development needs but also how to use one's strengths to leverage development. There are guides to help with analyzing one's network and using other people as resources, and a section devoted to the interaction between the boss and the developing person. In short, a person who takes this book seriously will end up with a serious development plan that, if carried out, will make a real difference. There is nothing superficial about the development plans that result from using these tools (though creating a plan is fun because the questions are interesting and there are frequent self-scoring questionnaires planted strategically along the way).

A final note about the authors. Both Paul and Mary are industrial-organizational psychologists, a fancy way of saying scientists who are trained to take a research-based approach to understanding people and organizations. Don't let the easy-to-digest way this book is written fool you. This material rests on a solid behavioral science foundation and years of intensive work on the part of the authors with unprecedented involvement by a large sample of managers and executives. It is a real testament to their skill that they have been able to translate the knowledge gained from their research into such a helpful collection of tools and guides for developing talent.

Morgan McCall,
Professor of Management and Organization,
Marshall School of Business,
University of Southern California

Series Editor's Preface

The *Talent Management Essentials* series presents state-of-the-art thinking on critical talent management topics ranging from global staffing, to career pathing, to engagement, to executive staffing, to performance management, to mentoring, to real-time leadership development. Authored by leading authorities and scholars on their respective topics, each volume offers state-of-the-art thinking and the epitome of evidence-based practice. These authors bring to their books an incredible wealth of experience working with small, large, public, and private organizations, as well as keen insights into the science and best practices associated with talent management.

Written succinctly and without superfluous "fluff," this series provides powerful and practical treatments of essential talent topics critical to maximizing individual and organizational health, well-being, and effectiveness. The books, taken together, provide a comprehensive and contemporary treatment of approaches, tools, and techniques associated with Talent Management. The goal of the series is to produce focused, prescriptive volumes that translate the data- and practice-based knowledge of I/O psychology and Organizational Behavior into practical, "how to" advice for dealing with cutting-edge organizational issues and problems.

Talent Management Essentials is a comprehensive, practitioner-oriented series of "best practices" for the busy solution-oriented manager, executive, HR leader, and consultant. And, in its application of evidence-based practice, this series will also appeal to professors, executive MBA students, and graduate students in Organizational Behavior, Human Resources Management, and I/O Psychology.

Steven Rogelberg

Preface

Your Job is the Classroom!

Research over the past two decades consistently indicates that over 70 percent of your development as a leader occurs on the job in trial-by-fire experiences that push you to the edge of your comfort zone.[1] The purpose of this book is to provide guidance and tools that you, as a line manager or human resource (HR) professional, can use to develop yourself, develop your team, and build an organization where leaders at *all* levels are using experience to drive their development.

We have called the book *Real Time Leadership Development* because we believe most development occurs in the moment – while leaders are running the business. Unfortunately, much of this learning is haphazard. Sometimes leaders pass up or overlook opportunities to accelerate their development. Sometimes they are in the right jobs but they are so busy running the business that the lessons pass them by. In the most unfortunate cases, they finish the experience and are worse leaders on the other side because they took away the wrong lessons. Our experience is that running the business and developing leadership capabilities are *not* two separate tasks; they can occur simultaneously *if* leaders put themselves into the right challenges, create rich learning environments, and pause long enough to make sure they are capturing the lessons along the way.

Furthermore, as a senior leader or HR professional, a big part of your job should be to develop future leaders in your organization, and you probably leave the office at night thinking that you are not doing enough. You know that you don't spend nearly enough time developing others or developing yourself. What would be really helpful is figuring out how to develop leaders and drive the business at the same time.

And you don't really have time to read a lot of books. What you really want is a resource with some straightforward ideas, based on research that cuts to the chase, puts key points in bold, and includes simple checklists you can use personally and pass on to others. You would like a book that is written in the language of leaders, not academics, so you don't have to translate the ideas but can focus on applying them. If you are in HR, you would like suggestions that complement and enhance your current talent management initiatives.

We have focused on general principles that will apply in a variety of situations, across multiple companies. We have avoided guidance that is contingent; that is, advice that is only applicable to leaders in certain types of companies or applicable in some situations but not others. There are, of course, many contingencies, but our book focuses on the ideas and actions that every leader should be considering as they think about their own development and the development of the leaders in their organization.

When considering development, leaders need to think and operate on three levels: (1) developing themselves, (2) developing their teams, and (3), if in a senior leadership role, developing managers throughout the organization. Good leaders model what they expect of others and this includes personal development. But modeling alone isn't enough. Leaders also need to think about and invest their time to develop the people who report to them. At senior levels, the challenge is to put systems in place that will develop strong leaders throughout the organization. In each chapter, we address all three of these levels with specific actions that can be taken at each of them.

To help accomplish this goal the chapters and tools in this book are written so they are "sneezeable"; that is, they are self-contained so you can easily pass them on to others, and they catch them like a cold. Our hope is that as the managers in your organization see these tools they can use the ideas to accelerate their development, and "sneeze" them to others who use them to develop the people around them. We have written chapters that are short, topical, and independent so you can focus on the subjects that are most important to you or, if interested, can read the book from front to back to develop a full understanding of real time leadership development. We have kept all these criteria in mind as we chose the topics and wrote the chapters. The chapters are designed to flow logically, but can be read in any order. In Part I: Building Your Leadership Pipeline, we discuss how, based on your business strategy, you can identify the experiences, competencies, and relationships that will be needed by future leaders in your organization. We finish this section with a discussion of the metrics that you can use to assess how effectively you are developing leaders and employees throughout your organization. In Part II: Capturing the Lessons, we discuss how leaders can capture the many lessons that are likely passing them by every day. We focus on how leaders can identify stretch assignments, navigate through them successfully, and emerge as better leaders on the other side. In Part III: Drawing on Other People, we focus on the critical role that other people can and should play in a leader's development. We discuss how leaders can get the most out of these relationships. In Part IV: Building Experiences into Talent Management, we discuss how to make sure all of your talent management systems support on-the-job development, and why it's important to do so. In Part V: Moving from Success to Significance, we address the question that all leaders eventually ask themselves: "Development for the sake of what?" Leadership, at its best, is never for its own sake. Leadership is always in relationship to others. Leaders want to make a difference, to do things that matter, to serve, and to have a lasting impact.

Within each chapter, you will find four sections: The Challenge, The Bottom Line, Taking Action, and To Learn More.

- *The Challenge.* Today's leaders and HR professionals face tremendous challenges. Almost all organizations today, big and small, are facing rapidly changing, complex environments. Organizations need employees who are able to grow and adapt to meet ever-changing demands. In this section, we discuss the challenges that you face in trying to develop yourself and others in such a fast-paced environment.
- *The Bottom Line.* In this section, we highlight the three to five most important things you need to know about the topic based on two criteria: (1) what does the research in industrial-organizational

(I-O) psychology tell us about this topic? and (2) what can you do that will make the greatest difference in your development and in the development of leaders in your organization?

- *Taking Action.* As every executive knows, knowledge by itself is never enough – action is ultimately what really matters. In this section, we discuss the actions that you can take personally, with your team, and in your organization to develop future talent. We address issues which affect both your development and the development and growth of others in your organization. Both are important for business success.
- *To Learn More*: Any of the topics discussed could be expanded into a whole book, and in fact, many of them are! Therefore, in each chapter, references are provided to deepen your expertise in the subject matter. We've focused on readings that are research-based and written for business leaders. We have included a mixture of books, articles, and in a few cases, interesting research studies.

We have worked to create a book that doesn't require you to add yet another task to your already busy day because, quite honestly, if you are like most leaders, there just isn't any room. Our hope is that the suggestions in the book can be easily integrated into the work you are already doing. For example, if you are a line manager, you might want to read a chapter every week and look for ways to incorporate it into your daily work. To develop your direct reports, you could give copies to your team, assigning and discussing selected chapters during your staff meetings. If you are an HR professional, the content is designed to complement your ongoing talent management processes. For example, this book could be given to leadership development program participants to promote continued development beyond the classroom. The checklists and tools throughout could be modified and adapted to enhance the performance management and employee development processes in your organization, moving the system from "some paperwork that HR says I have to do" to become a set of resources and tools that managers and employees *want* to use.

We hope you find the book helpful in your own development, in the development of your team, and in releasing the leadership potential in your organization.

Acknowledgements

We would like to thank our families: Sheryl, Jessica, and Jared Yost and Edward, Sean, and Colin Plunkett. Without their encouragement, support, and patience, this book would not have been written.

We would also like to thank all the leaders we have worked with over the years who have taught *us* about leadership development, especially Peter Morton, Lisa Saari, Tim Hall, Tanya Clemens, Joe Haupt, and Dave Ross. We would also like to thank Miller Adams, Mary Armstrong, Kelli Asbjornsen, Conrad Ball, Richard Baniak, Bill Baragar, Norm Bartlett, Rhonda Beaubien, Lisa Beers, Linda Bellerby, Roger Besancenez, Stephen Birell, Jim Biteman, Steven Bjorkman, Marian Black, Carla Bowman, Sheila Boze, Cheryl Braverman, Veronica Brooks, Greg Burton, Laura Cain, Mike Calandro, Christian Callahan, Ian Cannon, Jeffrey Caracillo, Leanne Caret, Teresa Carleton, Paul Cejas, Barbara Claitman, Linda Clarke, Daniel Collins, Garth Cook, Elizabeth Covert, Will Crawford, Cheryl Cunha, Marc DeBord, Jack Dougherty, Stephen Duffield, Clare Elser, Geoff Evans, Kim Failor, Kathy Fenster, Rich Finck, Pat Finneran, Jr., Gary Fleming, Marcella Fleming, Debbie Gavin, Mark Gonske, Theresa Hebert, Lissa Hollenbeck, Jeffrey Hutson, Bonnie Jackson, John Judy, Trish Kelley, Alan Kidd, Dale Kohn, Janice Krieg, Rocky Kuhns, Robert Kurtz, Jonathan Lee, Charlotte Lin, Mark Lodge, Scott Malcolm, Chris-Jon Marlette, Gerald Martin, Sharon Masterson, Mike Maurer, Stacy McCarthy, Ronald McClain, Reed Morren,

Patricia Mosier, Andrew Moskowitz, Janet Mower, Bill Munsch, Nancy Nicholas, Richard Noviello, Charlie O'Conner, James Ogonowski, Patricia Olsen, Mark Owen, Betty Pruitt, Velma Purser, Maria Randell, Rebecca Reason, Nancy Reeves, Melanie Reilly, Sandra Riley, Beanetta Roberts, Christopher Ross, Debbie Rub, Gail Sailer, Eric Sarkissian, Eric Schwartz, Sue Slattery, Tim Smith, Mike Stehno, Patricia Steinberg, John Steinmeyer, Roger Stropes, John Tarp, Bev Thompson, Suzi Tipton, Gordon Tucker, William Van Vleet III, Cynthia Vetsch, Ed Viau, Al Voss, Ken Westerfield, Michael Whipps, Janette Wilson, Susan Wirth, Christine Witte, Mike Woolley, Gina Woullard, Gary Wycoff, Ken Yata, Jim York, Bob Zibell, and David E. Zilz.

Special thanks to Steve Mercer who always challenged us to think bigger. We are grateful to Astha Parmar who provided valuable input on early drafts and the illustrations that appear in this book. We want to thank Glenna Chang who helped edit the final manuscript. And special thanks to the book series editor Steven Rogelberg for his insights during the process.

Our final thanks go to Morgan McCall. His research and thinking sparked our passion and commitment to ongoing leadership development. We consider our work part of his legacy.

Part I

Building Your Leadership Pipeline

If the research suggests that experience is the best teacher, then a leader's job is the best classroom. That makes the task of developing future leaders easy, right? Just throw your best and the brightest into tough assignments and see who survives on the other side. Unfortunately, this strategy leaves a lot of carnage along the way, including several people who might have made great senior leaders if they had been given the right assignments and the right kind of support. The costs don't stop there. "Survival of the fittest" as a succession management strategy guarantees that some of these leaders will damage the business on their way down and leave a hole in your leadership team. Ironically, the leaders who emerge on the other side won't necessarily be the ones you want. All you will know is that they survived *today's* challenges but you have little idea if they can meet *tomorrow's* challenges. In fact, they are more likely to get stuck in the past – a one-trick pony, relying on the skills that got them to where they are now. This strategy might be okay if you run a business in a static environment but this isn't the reality that most businesses face today.

Leadership development should be strategic, not random and unfocused. Haphazardly throwing leaders into stretch assignments is dangerous if you don't have a clear vision of the future. Leaders need to know what they should be learning to make the most of any developmental opportunities. Even if leaders never change jobs, they will invest their time and effort more productively if they are provided a framework they can use to think about their development; they will be able to focus on *experiences* in their jobs that are important, the leadership *competencies* that they will need, and the kinds of *relationships* that will best develop them as leaders. Each of these three topics will be covered in turn.

In Part I, we discuss how you can identify the types of leaders that you will need to meet current and future business challenges, and how you can systematically identify the job elements that will best develop those leaders. We discuss how you can use the business strategy to identify the leadership experiences, competencies, and relationships that future leaders will need. Each chapter includes several specific actions you can take to develop yourself, to develop the people who report to you, and – if you are a senior leader or HR professional – to develop leaders throughout your organization. We conclude Part I with some talent management metrics you can use to assess the strength of the leadership and professional talent in your organization.

Chapter 1

Linking Business Strategy and Experiences

The Challenge

If you are like most leaders, you worry about the leadership strength in your organization. For example, you might be confident that you have managers who can execute against the current strategy, but are worried that they are not prepared to take the business in new directions. You might have young leaders with lots of potential, but they lack the insight and wisdom that only experience can bring. Or maybe you are worried you don't have enough leaders who are ready to move into senior roles.

In the next three chapters, we discuss how you can identify the experiences, leadership competencies, and relationships that are most critical in the development of your future leaders. The three areas can be considered interrelated but distinct aspects of leadership development. Taken together, the experience, competency, and relationship taxonomies that you develop can become the framework that all leaders in the organizations can use to assess themselves and to identity what they can do to develop their leadership capabilities. We start with developmental experiences. Experiences are *where* leaders develop the competencies and the relationships that they need to be successful. The next question is obvious: What are the "right" experiences and where are they in my organization?

The Bottom Line

There are some simple, basic steps that you can take to identify the critical developmental experiences in your organization and turn the

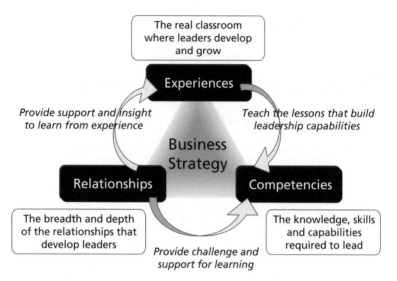

Figure 1.1 The foundations of leadership development

taxonomy into a set of tools that you, your team, and your organization can use to build future leadership capacity.

Start with the Business Strategy

The business strategy is always the place to begin. Most organizations already have this in place. If you are in a small company, everyone should know what this is. If you work in a division or department within a larger company, consider the role that your team plays in the overall strategy. If you don't have a strategy, take the time to work with your team to clearly define the business you are in and the value you provide.[1] Once you have a clear picture of where you are going, you can identify the kinds of leaders you will need to meet the future challenges and how future leaders will need to be different from the leaders you have in place today.

Don't Reinvent the Wheel

Your business strategy provides the context for what is important. Next, it's time to identify the experiences that will develop leaders who can achieve your business goals. Rather than trying to identify the experiences from scratch, start with the ones that have consistently emerged in research as the most critical in the development of leaders (see box below).

Find the Experiences that are Unique to Your Organization

Once you understand the business strategy and have reviewed the experiences in the box above, work with senior executives in the organization and/or members of your team to identify the 10–20 experiences that are most important in *your* organization. Several of the experiences are likely

---

Good to Know:
Core Leadership Development Experiences

Below are some of the experiences that have consistently emerged as key events in the development of leaders.[2]

First supervisory position: the first time a leader is formally required to manage a team and get things done through other people.

Start-ups: launching a new business venture and experiencing all of the phases of building a business from scratch.

Turning a business around: fixing or stabilizing a failing business.

Key business units or functional experience: experience in a key business unit or function within the organization. For example, in a technology company, this might include managing software developers. In a manufacturing company, this might include managing a production line.

Managing a larger scope: a significant increase in scope that includes expanding the functions or business lines being managed or moving to a more senior leadership level (e.g., moving from functional to business unit management) that requires advanced and significantly different leadership capabilities.[3]

Good/bad role models: exposure to a particularly good or bad role model. Most often this will be bosses but could include personal role models outside of work.

Lateral transitions: moving from a line position (e.g., leading a business unit) to a staff role (e.g., moving to corporate headquarters) or vice versa. This may also include moving from

Continued

---

one department to another that is significantly different (e.g., from manufacturing to sales and service).

Failures/mistakes: experiencing a significant failure or mistake and learning the lessons that come with it.

Dealing with a problem employee: managing a poorly performing employee, including the need in many cases to eventually fire the person. This may be the first time a manager has to fire someone, or the removal of a highly visible senior leader later in one's career.

Significant career change: significant transitions in one's career such as taking a large career risk, moving to a new organization, or moving to a new industry.

Leadership training and development: participating in an executive and leadership development program, a job rotation program, or the pursuit of an advanced degree.

Personal life events: having experienced powerful personal events, outside of work, that led to a significant change in one's approach to leadership including *traumatic events* such as illness, divorce, or the death of a family member or *positive events* such as early childhood experiences, student leadership, becoming a parent, or community service.

Global experience: working and living outside one's home country in a job that requires leading people, teams, and organizations in a culture significantly different from one's own.

to be the same ones listed in the box, but others are likely to be unique to your business. For example, some of the unique experiences might include holding a leadership position in one of the key business units or functions or geographical locations specific to your organization. In an information technology (IT) company like Microsoft, critical experiences might include time in a technical leadership role, time in a sales and service leadership position, or experience in a global assignment. In a manufacturing company like Boeing, spending time in the commercial airplane and in the defense industry parts of the business will be important experiences for senior leaders.

Use the questions in the box below to identify the key experiences in your organization or department. In a larger company, interview senior executives to identify a short list of experiences. In medium to large organizations an HR professional can support this effort. In a smaller organization or within a single department, the senior leader of the group could simply meet with his or her leadership team to create the list.

Tips:
Identifying Key Experiences in Your Organization

The following questions can be used to identify the experiences that are most critical in the development of leaders in *your* organization. Talk to senior executives and other people who understand the current and future challenges facing the company. Other people to interview might include leaders working directly with key customers, high potential leaders in key business functions and geographies, and people in the strategy department.

Business Strategy

- What makes this company successful (e.g., what is its sustainable, strategic advantage)?
- What kinds of leaders are needed today and what kinds of leaders will be needed in the future to maintain this advantage?
- What are the key business challenges that the company will face in the next three to five years? What are the experiences that will prepare leaders to face these challenges?

Key Experiences

- What were the critical experiences in your development as a leader? Of those, which ones will continue to be critical for the next generation of leaders? What new experiences will be critical for the next generation of leaders?
- What business unit and/or functional experience will senior leaders need to meet future challenges?
- Of these experiences, which ones should come first; that is, which experiences are most important in the development of a leader early in his or her career?
- Which should come later; that is, which ones require the leader to be in a more senior position to get the full benefit of the experience?
- What else would you like to add?

Define the Experiences

The experiences need to be defined in enough depth for leaders to be able to use the definitions to assess themselves. For example, for a global experience to be most powerful, do leaders need to live in another country for it to "count" or can they manage global suppliers while living in their home country? How long do they have to be in the experience to really learn the lessons? What leadership capabilities should they develop in the experience and what lessons should they learn? The next box provides the kind of information that is important to include. The best way to develop the final definitions is to assign both a line leader and an HR partner the task. The line leader ensures that the language is right (e.g., relevant and business-focused). The HR partner ensures that the content is consistent with best practices and aligned with the talent management processes in the company.

Taking Action

To fully leverage the power of experience-based development, you will need to take action at three levels: (1) What can you do to develop yourself? (2) What can you do to develop your team? (3) If you are a senior leader or HR professional, what can you do to develop leaders in your organization? We will challenge you to consider these three levels in every chapter in this book.

Get Started

Don't wait for the company to do this for you. Start with your business and your team. Create a list of key experiences that are critical in *your* department and for the development of *your* team members. Make sure you take the time to identify both the experiences that are required now and the ones that will be increasingly important in the future. Then look for ways that you can help the larger organization consider how to use on-the-job-experience to more systematically develop future leaders' potential.

Example:
The Start Up Experience – An Experience Description

Start-up experiences that are the most developmental require leaders to launch *new* products or services, or take an established product/service in a completely new direction. The best experiences require the leader to build the team from scratch, identify and develop a new business model, interact directly with customers, build the processes and infrastructure to support the new product/service, and assess the ongoing commercial potential of the offering in order to adapt to emerging market conditions.

Depth of Experience

The following descriptions can be used to assess the depth of the experience.

Low: The leader is in a junior leadership position in a start-up venture with limited authority/responsibility for delivering the business products or services. The experience lasts for a limited period of time (e.g., one year or less), allowing the leader to work only through limited phases of the start-up life cycle (e.g., business model definition, building the team, product/service development, market pricing/positioning strategy, or experiencing success/failure). The leader participates in a quasi-start-up experience such as building a new team or department from scratch, launching a new internal process with tight deadlines, launching an upgrade to an existing product/service, or becoming a sales/service manager in a new geography.

Moderate: The leader is in a senior leadership role with shared authority/responsibility for delivering the business products or services. The experience lasts for a moderate amount of time (e.g., one to two years) requiring the leader to work through several start-up stages (e.g., business model definition, building the team, product/service development, market pricing/positioning strategy, experiencing success/failure).

Significant: The leader is in a senior leadership role with primary authority/responsibility for delivering the business products or services. The experience lasts for a significant amount of time (e.g., two or more years) requiring the leader to work through all of the start-up stages (e.g., business model definition, building the team, product/service development, market pricing/positioning strategy, experiencing success/failure).

Navigating the Experience

Start-up experiences are simultaneously exciting and daunting. Successfully navigating through them requires a drive to succeed, risk tolerance,

Continued

adaptability, persistence, and the ability to build a team that complements the leader's skill set and makes up for the leader's weaknesses. The most intense developmental start-up experiences require the leader to lead a team into uncharted territory, building the team and infrastructure from scratch, under moderate to high time pressure, with low interdependency with other parts of the organization, a rapid development and release cycle time, and high customer contact and feedback.

Competencies Developed/Lessons Learned

Some of the key lessons to look for in a start-up include strategic thinking, ability to communicate and sell a vision, the failure points and keys to success in the early stages, business acumen, building and leveraging a network, driving execution, risk tolerance, customer relations, technical skills, and self-confidence.

Metrics to Watch

Metrics to assess leadership performance in a start-up include expenditures versus budget, time to market, cash flow, trends in market share, customer satisfaction, and trends in profitability. Leadership development metrics to watch include team member retention rates, employee survey scores, and 360-feedback ratings (i.e., feedback from a person's manager, peers, direct reports, and sometimes from outside sources). Because start-ups are so dynamic, informal customer and coworker feedback can play an especially critical role in the leader's ability to adapt, develop, and perform.

Further Reading on Start-Ups

Christensen, C. M. (2003). *The innovator's solution: Creating and sustaining successful growth*. Boston, MA: Harvard Business School Press.
Drucker, P. F. (1985). *Innovation and entrepreneurship: Practice and principles*. New York: Harper & Row.
McGrath, R. G., & MacMillan, I. (2000). *The entrepreneurial mindset*. Boston, MA: Harvard Business School Press.

Assess Yourself

Once your list of key experiences is developed, reflect on your own development: Which of these experiences have you had and which ones are you missing? What experience are you in right now? What should you be learning? How will you know if you have improved in these areas? What will you see? What are the experiences that will make you an even better leader in the future?

Assess Your Team

Consider the experiences that the members of your team are in right now: What should they be learning? What are they learning? In what ways should they be different leaders a year from now? Have you discussed this with them? How can you help them navigate through the challenges? Now look ahead: What are the future experiences that your direct reports need in their development? Rather than sending them to training next year, what are some assignments you could give them in the coming year that would build their capabilities?

Build the Experiences into Your Organization's Talent Management Systems

Whether you are a senior executive or an HR leader, the experiences can become one of your key tools to drive experience-based development into the whole organization. The taxonomy of key experiences should be built into all of the talent management processes in your organization. For example, the taxonomy of experiences could be used in the succession planning process to more systematically consider future job assignments for aspiring leaders. In the same way, the list of experiences can be made available to *all* leaders during annual career development discussions to help them think more systematically about their development. More ideas about how you can build experience-based development into your talent management processes are discussed in Part IV.

What is the Best Order for the Experiences?

We are often asked if there is an optimal order to development assignments (e.g., how should they be sequenced?) and are specific assignments important for specific roles (e.g., CFO)? Unfortunately the only definitive answer to these questions is: The type and sequence of any development assignments, for any role in your organization, must be centered on your organization's business strategy. So we cannot be prescriptive. If your business strategy involves expanding existing product lines into emerging markets, then one set of development assignments will be important. If the organization is focused on developing and selling new products to existing customers, then a different set will be required. An early cross-cultural assignment along with opportunities to leverage operational excellence (e.g., turn around a poorly performing product line) would be advisable in the first instance; perhaps nonvalue-added for the second.

To Learn More

The following books provide guidance on the experiences that tend to be the most powerful in the development of leaders and the lessons they teach:

Charan, R., Drotter, S., & Noel, J. L. (2001). *The leadership pipeline: How to build the leadership-powered company.* San Francisco: John Wiley & Sons.

Dotlich, D. L., Noel, J. L., & Walker, N. (2004). *Leadership passages: The personal and professional transitions that make or break a leader.* San Francisco, CA: Jossey-Bass.

Lombardo, M. M., & Eichinger, R. W. (1988). *Eighty-eight assignments for development in place.* Greensboro, NC: Center for Creative Leadership.

McCall, M. W., & Hollenbeck, G. P. (2002). *Developing global executives.* Boston, MA: Harvard Business School Press.

McCall, M. W., Lombardo, M. M., & Morrison, A. M. (1988). *The lessons of experience: How successful executives develop on the job.* New York: The Free Press.

Chapter 2

Linking Business Strategy and Competencies

The Challenge

Leaders are often clear about the performance expected of their employees but fail to clearly articulate what people should be learning in their current assignments. They don't assess whether employees are capturing the right lessons or developing the right leadership competencies along the way. Maybe the critical leadership competencies have never been clearly articulated in your business. In the last chapter, we outlined a process you can use to identify the experiences that will develop the next generation of leaders in your organization. In this chapter, we'll discuss how you can reliably and validly identify the leadership competencies that are developed in each of the experiences.

The Bottom Line

Begin with What We Already Know About Leadership

Over the last several decades, industrial-organizational (I-O) psychologists have conducted research to identify the traits, behaviors, and competencies that are most strongly related to leadership effectiveness. The research suggests that there are a consistent set of characteristics that affect who chooses to step into a leadership role, who is chosen as the leader, and how well that leader performs. Some of the characteristics that appear to be particularly important include a

Figure 2.1 The foundations of leadership development

strong desire to lead, intelligence, drive and energy, openness to new experiences, emotional stability and maturity, self-confidence, and a high internal sense of control.[1] Other leadership competencies tend to develop and mature over time: skills like business acumen, strategic thinking, effective team-building, negotiation skills, and the ability to work across organizations. Over time, I-O psychologists have defined, tested, and built behavioral definitions for the more important leadership competencies. References for some of the more commonly used leadership competency taxonomies are provided at the end of this chapter.

Leaders are Born and Made

Most organizations are too quick to label people as good or bad leaders. One of the biggest mistakes that organizations can make is to assume that people either have leadership potential or they don't. Recent research suggests that genetic factors account for about 30 percent of leadership emergence (who becomes a leader) and leadership level (the level of management that people attain – e.g., first-level, mid-level, or executive-level leadership positions).[2] Leadership personality traits might get someone noticed, but they need to be refined and developed in the fires of experience. Considerable research suggests that competencies develop, grow, and emerge over time and play out in different ways in different situations.[3] Some things that we think of as very stable, like personality or intelligence, can change over time.[4] There is no linear or predictable path to great leadership. Leaders can move up, move laterally, and even fall backwards on their path forward (for example, you might have noticed in the last chapter that failures/mistakes consistently emerge as one of the critical experiences in the development of leaders). Thus judging leaders too early is a dangerous business. Some people may be genetically more likely to emerge and be successful in leadership positions; *however*, the best leaders are ultimately developed in the continuous stretch, tumble, and bump of the real world.

Consider Your Business Strategy

It is important to find the competencies that are most important in *your* organization. Your business strategy defines the kinds of leaders that you need and what they need to be able to do. In addition to the core leadership traits listed earlier, every company will have unique competencies that are important. If you work in a large company, an organization-wide set of leadership competencies may have already been defined and you can use them. If you have to develop them from scratch, it can be a complicated and time-consuming process, especially if the competencies will be used for selection or promotion decisions. Developing a fair, valid, and legally defensible set of competencies requires someone with strong technical expertise who uses a rigorous process that follows well-established, research-based methods and conforms to legal requirements.[5] If you are a line manager, your best strategy is to work closely with your HR and legal departments to develop the competencies. You have more freedom if you are just using them to help develop leaders on your team and aren't using them to make promotional or selection decisions. If there isn't any company-wide list of leadership competencies, a simple first step is to start with the competencies listed in one of the books at the end of this chapter and work with your team to identify the ones that are most important in your organization. You also might interview senior leaders in your organization to identify what they consider most important. Questions are provided in the box below to get the process started.

Tips:
Identifying Key Leadership Competencies in Your Organization

The following questions can be used to identify the competencies that are most critical in the development of leaders in *your* organization. Talk to senior executives and other people who understand the current and future challenges facing the company. Other people to interview might include leaders working directly with key customers, high potential leaders in key business functions and geographies, and people in the strategy department.

Business Strategy

• What makes this company successful (e.g., what is its sustainable, strategic advantage)?
• What kinds of leaders are needed today and what kinds of leaders will be needed in the future to maintain this advantage?
• What are the key business challenges the company will face in the next three to five years? What are the leadership competencies that leaders will need to face these challenges?

Leadership Competencies

• What differentiates the outstanding versus typical leaders in the organization?
• Think of two people you know who you would say have the potential to be strong future leaders within this organization. What differentiates these people from other leaders?
• What leadership competencies and capabilities are missing in the current leadership team?
• What competencies are good but are not at the levels they need to be?
• What competencies are not required now, but will be critical for future leaders?
• How will future leaders need to be different from you?

Finalize the List of Competencies, Define Them, and Validate Them

Left to our own devices, we are terrible judges of other people. The selection research suggests that, without rigorous assessment methods, managers' judgments in situations like job interviews tend to be no better than chance. The same is true for leadership development. The steps listed above can be used to identify the types of traits and competencies that are most important for leaders in your organization; however, simply creating a list of leadership competencies isn't enough. The competencies should be defined in enough detail that leaders can assess themselves against them. The definitions should define different levels of the competency (e.g., basic skills, moderate skills, and advanced skills) so leaders can self-assess their current levels versus where they want to be, or need to be, in the future. The definitions should be behavioral and observable. The next box provides a sample behaviorally anchored definition for the competency "thinking strategically." Well-defined competencies become a great tool for a variety of purposes. They can be used by leaders as a self-assessment to identify the areas where they are strong and weak. Then they can be used in combination with experiences to help leaders identify work assignments that will develop the leader, and eventually used by the leader and the organization to assess whether or not development has actually occurred.

Map the Key Experiences to the Leadership Competencies

In the previous chapter, you identified key experiences that are important for leadership development. Your next task is to think about the linkages between the experiences and competencies, that is: Which competencies are developed in each of the experiences? A simple way to do this is to create a matrix mapping the competencies that are developed in each of the experiences (see Table 2.1). Previous research and interviews with current leaders can be combined to build your matrix. For example, the original research conducted by the Center for Creative Leadership and discussed in their book *The Lessons of Experience* identifies 16 key experiences and the lessons learned in each.[6] To validate and customize this to your organization, a team of successful leaders and leadership development professionals could use this information to create a matrix for your organization. If you want to be more rigorous, consider interviewing senior leaders in your company, asking them to identify key events in their development and the lessons they learned or competencies they developed in each. An even more rigorous approach would be to send a survey to a wider sample of leaders in the organization, asking them

---

Example:
Competency Definitions

Organizations use a variety of methods to define and scale competencies. Some organizations create them by leadership level, for example, defining the behaviors that first-level, mid-level, and executive-level leaders will need. The disadvantage of this method is that job roles often dictate competency requirements more accurately than management levels (e.g., the first-level manager in the strategy organization will need a high level of strategic thinking skills). Instead, we recommend that you consider defining proficiency levels for each competency that is unrelated to organizational level (see the example below). This allows the proficiency levels to be tailored and assigned for different leaders in different roles in different parts of the organization. In this way, high strategic thinking proficiency levels can be required for all leaders in the strategy group independent of their management level.

Thinking Strategically

Level 1: Ability to: translate corporate strategy into team goals; analyze and think through cause/effect relationships; analyze and solve immediate problems; and consider actions and strategies within a one-year time horizon.

Level 3: Ability to: influence corporate strategic goals as an expert in his or her discipline, function, or business unit; consider several factors simultaneously and draw out the effects they are likely to have on one another; solve immediate problems in ways that will also prevent future problems; and consider the impact of actions and strategies within a three- to five-year time horizon.

Level 5: Ability to: develop strategy in a major area of the business while considering external factors (e.g., economic conditions, government regulations, and population trends) and internal capabilities (e.g., corporate strengths, weaknesses, resources); consider multiple factors that interact and change dynamically over time and identify a subset of levers that will drive the desired results; consider how to solve immediate problems in ways that will increase the organization's ability to solve a broad range of problems in the future; and consider the impact of actions and strategies on the organization five or more years out.

Table 2.1 Key Experiences and the Leadership Competencies They Develop (Example)

	Strategic thinking	Business acumen	Customer commitment	Driving results	Building organizational systems	Building effective teams	Working across organizations	Leading globally	Technical expertise
Business experiences									
Start-up business	●	●	●	O	O	●			
Sustaining business		●	O	O	O	●	O		
Turnaround business	O	●	O	●	●				
Discipline experiences									
Engineering/technical leadership			O	O			O		●
Sales & marketing leadership	O	●	O						
Line leadership position	●	●	●	O	O				
Corporate staff positions							●		O
Perspective building experiences									
Role models						●	O		
Strategic task force	O			O			O		
Global experience			O				O	●	

● = Primary Lessons
O = Secondary Lessons

to identify the key events in their development and the competencies they learned in each.

Once the matrix is created, leaders can use it to identify the experience they are in and the lessons they should be learning (moving horizontally across the row), or they can identify the competencies they want to develop and then look for the kinds of experiences that will best develop those competencies (moving down the column).

Taking Action

Identify the Leadership Competencies That are Most Important in Your Organization

Take the time to identify the leadership competencies that are most important in your organization. If you are in charge of a department and the larger organization already has a standard set of leadership competencies, spend some time discussing with your team the ones on the list that are particularly important in your business. If the larger organization hasn't identified a list, use the books listed in the "To Learn More" section at the end of this chapter to identify the leadership competencies that are particularly important for your business. As you look at the lists, consider which ones are most important now and which ones will be important in the future. Look for the areas where leaders tend to be strong and where there are worrying gaps.

Assess Yourself and Your Team

Once the competency list has been established, measure yourself against the list. Where are *you* strong? Where do *you* need to develop and grow? What competencies will become even more important in the future? Once you have assessed yourself, consider the members of your team. Where are they strong? Where are they weak? Challenge your team members to assess themselves against the competencies, and then have a discussion as a team. Make sure the discussions focus on strengths *and* weaknesses rather than just weaknesses alone. For example, one of your direct reports may show promise in networking across departments, a strength which could be enhanced to become an even stronger asset for this person in the future.

Find the Experiences That Will Develop the Required Competencies

Assessing yourself is only the first step. The next step is to take action to develop in the areas where you are weak. That means putting yourself in situations and assignments that will challenge you to grow. And, as a leader, it means working with your direct reports to find assignments and projects that will stretch them and challenge them to grow. Use the experiences–competencies grid that you created to identify future assignments that will challenge them to learn new skills. If you are a senior leader or the HR professional in charge of talent management, make the grid part of the development planning process and challenge all leaders in the company to use it. The grid is a way to promote on-the-job development over classroom training by giving leaders a tool they can use to identify the projects and assignments that will develop their leadership potential.

Build the Leadership Competencies Into Your Organization's Talent Management Systems

The leadership competencies that you identify are worthless until they are used. It is important to weave them into your business strategy and your talent management systems. For example, they could be integrated into the succession management process to help strategically place leaders in assignments that will help them develop in areas where they are weak. Imagine a leader who is great at implementation and execution, but needs to demonstrate an ability to think more strategically in order to be promoted to the next level. Your competency-experience grid tells you that sending that leader to China to expand your current line of products is a great way for him or her to deepen strategic thinking. Moreover, in the process the leader is also likely to learn complementary skills like global thinking, building networks, and leading in the midst of ambiguity. By using this framework, identifying the competencies which can be learned from each key experience, and providing relational support along the way, you can develop your leaders while keeping an intense focus on growing your company.

Part IV provides more guidance on how you can better integrate competencies, experiences, and key relationships into your talent management processes. The important point here is this: as the HR or business leader, you obviously can't work closely with every leader, so you need to create a framework that aspiring leaders can use to strategically guide their own development. Clearly identifying the experiences, the leadership competencies, and the linkages between the two provides proactive leaders with the means to guide their development.

To Learn More

A comprehensive review of the research on leadership and leadership development can be found in:

Yukl, G. (2006). *Leadership in organizations*, 6th edn. Upper Saddle River, NJ: Prentice-Hall.

Leadership competency taxonomies developed by I-O psychologists and used in many companies can be found in the following texts:

Byham, W. C., Smith, A. B., & Paese, M. J. (2002). *Grow your own leaders: How to identify, develop, and retain leadership talent.* Upper Saddle River, NJ: Development Dimensions International Inc. & Prentice-Hall.

Gebelein, S. H., Stevens, L. A., Skube, C. J., Lee, D. G., Davis, B. L., & Hellervik, L. W. (2000). *Successful manager's handbook.* Minneapolis, MN: Personnel Decisions International.

Lombardo, M. W., & Eichinger, R. W. (2001). *For your improvement: A development and coaching guide.* Minneapolis, MN: Lominger Limited, Inc.

For previous work that has been done linking experiences with the lessons learned, see:

Lombardo & Eichinger (2001). *For your improvement.*

McCall, M. W., Lombardo, M. M., & Morrison, A. M. (1988). *The lessons of experience: How successful executives develop on the job.* New York: The Free Press.

Chapter 3

Linking Business Strategy and Relationships

The Challenge

In the last two chapters, we discussed how to identify the experiences and the competencies that leaders will need to meet future business challenges. But leadership isn't simply a matter of how much you know. Leaders, by definition, get things done through other people. A leader's effectiveness also depends on the quality of the relationships they have built with key stakeholders inside and outside of the organization. Strong relationships build trust. Weak or poor relationships build barriers and resistance. Unfortunately, most organizations seldom give their leaders a roadmap to identify the kinds of relationships that are most important. Leaders are left to find their own way, often by trial and error. Some leaders have a natural ability to figure out "how things really work around here." Most leaders have to work at it. In this chapter, we'll discuss how you can identify the relationships that are most important in your development and the development of leaders in your organization.

The Bottom Line

Times are Changing

While relationships have been an informal part of talent management forever, strategically leveraging relationships to develop future leaders is a new frontier.[1] Historically, building leadership relationships

Figure 3.1 The foundations of leadership development

meant making sure you were part of the "old boy" network. But times are changing. People and organizations are more connected than ever. Leadership today is about knowing how to design an organization where groups of individuals are connected and working with the right people, where the organization is so tightly linked with the external environment that it can sense and respond to changes quickly, where the right decisions are being made as quickly as possible and as close to the customer as possible, and where the system can adapt and evolve over time. Leaders in this new world need to know who the key stakeholders are and be able to see the world from different perspectives.

Know the Relationships that Matter

All relationships are important! After all, leaders can only get things done *with* and *through* other people. You need to work with a wide *variety* of people to grow as a leader. However, a few relationships are going to be particularly critical in the development of senior leaders in your company – but which ones? Research suggests that two classes of relationships are particularly important: (1) working closely with a broad range of key stakeholder groups inside and outside of the organizations; and (2) building a network of developmental relationships.

Work with key stakeholder groups inside and outside the organization. Leaders need to build relationships that will help them understand the business from a variety of perspectives. That is, they need to build strong working relationships with key groups inside and outside of the organization. Henry Mintzberg, currently at McGill University, and a pioneer in the study of leadership, identified the following groups as key stakeholders in most organizations: the board of directors, top management, the owners (e.g., shareholders), the operators (i.e., employees who do the frontline work), line managers, staff groups (e.g., finance, legal, IT, HR, etc.), suppliers, partners, competitors, clients, employee associations (e.g., unions, professional organizations), and private/public agencies (e.g., local, national and international governments, special interest groups, opinion leaders, families).[2] Each group has a unique perspective on the organization. To succeed, leaders need to understand, partner with, and leverage these stakeholder groups to drive change in a complex and interdependent system. But building these relationships and understanding the different perspectives they bring takes time. That's why it is so valuable for organizations to identify and define the relationships so aspiring leaders can systematically look for and develop the relationships over the life of their careers.

Build a network of ongoing developmental relationships. Several ongoing relationships are particularly critical in the development of leaders.[3] In particular, managers, role models, and mentors play vital roles. These three relationships are so important that we have devoted separate chapters to discuss each of them in depth. For example, it should come as no surprise that bosses directly impact the ongoing development of employees.[4] Bosses can provide, or withhold, the resources, stretch opportunities, challenge, and support needed for development. In the same way, good and bad role models, mentors, and career champions – senior leaders who support aspiring leaders in the organization – can have an equally powerful impact on the development of a leader over the life of his or her career.[5] Even bad bosses can be powerful developmental experiences![6] Strong organizations create a culture where these kinds of relationships are built into leaders' everyday work and they encourage leaders to leverage these kinds of the developmental relationships.

Example:
Critical Relationships in Leadership Development

External

- Board of directors
- Key customers (business-to-business and end users)
- Key suppliers
- Business partners
- Government (international, national, state, and local)
- Industry/professional organizations
- Labor unions
- Media organizations

Internal

- Top management
- Business unit leaders
- Functional/staff leaders
- Country/regional executives
- Technical experts (e.g., senior engineers, scientists, economists)

Developmental

- Mentors
- Role models
- Current and former managers
- Current and former colleagues and direct reports

Find the Relationships That are Most Important in Your Organization

Once you have considered the criteria discussed above, you can begin to build the list of relationships that are most critical in your organization. The example above provides a generic list of the relationships that are important in most large organizations. In small organizations, everyone knows everyone, so external relationships (e.g., with key customers) become more critical. The next box provides a list of questions you can use to identify the unique internal and external relationships that are most important in your organization.

Based on these questions (and the research discussed above), create a draft list of the critical relationships in your organization. Then validate the final list with senior leaders to ensure it is accurate and complete. The conversations alone are likely to be a great catalyst to help leaders think more strategically and concretely about their personal networks.

Tips:
Finding the Critical Relationships in Your Organization

The following questions are designed to uncover the critical relationships in *your* organization. The people you talk to might include senior executives and other people who recognize the current and future challenges facing the company. These might include, among others, leaders working directly with key customers, high potential leaders in key business units, functions, and geographies, and people in the strategy group.

Business Strategy

- What are the key business challenges the company will face in the next three to five years? What makes this company successful (e.g., what is its sustainable, strategic advantage)?
- What kinds of leaders are needed today and what kinds of leaders will be needed in the future to maintain this advantage?
- What are the relationships that leaders will need to face these challenges?

Key External Relationships

- What relationships do future senior leaders need to establish with members of the organization's board of directors? What types of external boards should future seniors leaders consider serving on?

Continued

- Who are your key business-to-business customers (i.e., the organizations who directly purchase your products/services)? Who are your key end user customer groups (i.e., the ones who ultimately use your products/services)? Of these groups, which ones should every leader be exposed to? What kind and level of exposure would be most developmental for leaders?
- Who are the key suppliers to your organization? What kind and level of exposure would be most developmental for leaders?
- Who are the key business partners with your organization? What kind and level of exposure would be most developmental for leaders?
- Who are the key labor unions in your organization? What type of exposure and what level of relationships would be important to develop strong leaders in your organization?
- What government agencies and regulatory bodies (e.g., international, national, state, and local) can significantly impact your business?
- What industry or professional groups are particularly important to your organization's success?
- What other external organizations can significantly impact the success of your organization?

Key Internal Relationships

- What are the most important business units, functional departments, and geographies in the organization? Which ones will become even more important in the future?
- Which leaders are seen as role models in your organization? Which leaders are recognized as great mentors? What makes them so effective?
- What technical groups inside the company are critical to the organization's success? Are there any experts who are especially recognized for their technical expertise?

Assess the Relationships

To move development to an even higher level, create tools that leaders can use to assess the strength – breadth and depth – of the relationships they have built. Leaders can assess the *breadth* of their relationships by identifying the span of key groups they have worked with. Leaders also need to assess the *depth* of these relationships. Meeting customers is one thing, working with them on a daily basis over a two-year period is quite another. Each relationship can be scaled. An example scale for customer relationships appears below. The advantage of defining the depth of relationships is that it establishes a bar against which leaders can measure themselves. Clearly defining the depth and breadth that is expected helps both the leader and the organization identify serious gaps in a leader's development. Obviously, leaders won't need to be at the highest level in every relationship, but the structure provides a framework to help leaders think about where they can *best* direct their developmental efforts in the future.

Example:
Relationship Definitions

Customer Relationships (Business-to-Business): Establishing relationships with businesses that distribute the organization's products or services.

Low: Direct contact with low- or mid-level leaders in the customer organization, infrequent interaction (every other month), limited feedback from the customer about the organization's products/services, primarily a one-way relationship from your organization to the customer, interactions primarily with one department in the customer organization (e.g., accounting, sales, service, IT).

Moderate: Direct contact with mid-level leaders or higher in the customer organization, frequent interaction (at least once a week), moderate feedback about your organization's products/services, interactions with at least two departments in the customer organization (e.g., accounting, sales, service, IT).

Strong: Direct contact with multiple leadership levels including senior leaders in the customer organization, frequent interaction (at least once a week), rich feedback about the organization's products/services (e.g., strengths/weaknesses, future opportunities/threats), an interdependent relationship, interactions with several groups in the customer organization (e.g., accounting, sales, service, IT).

Taking Action

Get Started

Don't wait for the company to act. If your organization hasn't identified the critical relationships, start with your business and your team. Create a list of the relationships that are critical in your development and the development of your team members. Remember to include relationships that aren't necessarily important now but will be important in the future.

Assess Yourself and Your Team

Once you have created the list, assess yourself against it. How deep and how broad are your relationships? Where do you need to develop? Consider your team. Assess each of them against this list and challenge them to assess themselves. Find ways to use current and future projects to start building or deepening these relationships for yourself and your team members. You might set aside time during one of your team meetings to have this discussion or make it part of your development conversations with each of them.

To illustrate how a relationship framework could be used, consider the following example. Imagine that you have a leader with great potential whom you want to develop. She has been in the central finance group. Her next step is to run a product division in the company. When she takes over the job, you sit down with her and, using the framework, identify the relationships that will be most critical in the new role and why they are so important. In her new role, she will learn how to work with senior leaders, retail organizations, one of the company's key suppliers, and government regulators. You also connect her with a mentor who has been through a similar process and can provide both support and advice along the way.

Build the Relationships into Your Organization's Talent Management Systems

Very few talent management systems formally assess aspiring leaders on the breadth and depth of their relationships. If it is done at all, it's usually done after the fact (e.g., "We need to get John in front of the board of directors"). When critical relationships are discussed, the conversation is seldom specific enough to lead to concrete actions. Identifying and defining the key relationships allows both the organization and the leaders themselves to systematically assess development gaps. For example, the list can be integrated into and used to enhance the succession management process. High potential programs can make relationship development an integral part of the process.

To Learn More

The following references highlight some of the most important relationships in the development of leaders (see also the references in Part III):

Ibarra, H., & Hunter, M. (2007). How leaders create and use networks, *Harvard Business Review* **85(1)**, 40–7.

McCauley, C. D., & Douglas, C. A. (2004). Developmental relationships. In C. D. McCauley & E. Van Velsor (eds.), *Handbook of leadership development* (2nd edn, pp. 85–115), Greensboro, NC: Center for Creative Leadership.

Mintzberg, H. (1983). *Power in and around organizations*. Englewood Cliffs, NJ: Prentice Hall.

Chapter 4

Talent Management Metrics to Watch

The Challenge

Leaders face hundreds of metrics that cry out for their attention – revenue, income, earnings per share, cash flow, return on assets (ROA), sales growth, time to market for new products/services, customer satisfaction scores, and employee safety rates, to name only a few. None of these get done without the right people in place. Organizations are increasingly realizing the importance of tracking the leadership and professional talent in their organization. This includes the strength of current talent and the development of future talent. There are two categories of metrics that are particularly important to track: (1) *leadership bench strength* – the extent to which the right leaders are in place today, and the leaders needed for tomorrow are being developed; and (2) *organizational talent management* – the extent to which the organization is attracting, engaging, developing, and retaining key talent in its broader workforce.

There are a variety of metrics that organizations can use to assess these two dimensions. In this chapter we will discuss how you can identify and develop a short list of metrics to assess the leadership bench strength and employee talent in your organization. We also will highlight several measurement issues you should consider as you choose the metrics and how you can use the metrics to drive positive change in your organization.

The Bottom Line

Keep it Simple

Talent management metrics can get complicated. Organizations typically face one of two challenges: They proactively track very few, if any talent management metrics, or they have too many metrics. In the first case, readily available metrics may be simple and fairly useless numbers like training course completion rates. Metrics like attrition rates may be tracked in the HR database but not easy to obtain. Other organizations might track too much, often in different systems. They might track employee survey scores, turnover rates, recruiting spend, leadership competency ratings, performance appraisal scores, compensation, and so forth. They face an equally formidable challenge: What is the most important information in the midst of all the data?

The good news is that your best strategy is to keep it as simple as possible and track as few metrics as possible. Let's cut to the chase. Some of the best metrics to assess the strength of *your leadership pipeline* are:

- *Leadership bench strength*: Identify the key leadership roles in your organization and the number of candidates who are prepared to assume that role if it becomes available. You also might want to calculate the number of candidates who are "almost ready" for the role (e.g., one year or one move away). Organizational leadership bench strength can be computed by calculating the average number of "ready now" and "almost ready" leaders across the company. For example, let's say an organization finds that there are an average of 1.1 leaders who are "ready now" and 1.8 leaders who are "almost ready" across the key leadership roles in the company. This should raise some red flags. It suggests that if people leave you don't have a lot of viable in-house options to fill critical roles (e.g., you only have one person on average in back-up positions). This will be especially problematic if the same back-up people appear as likely candidates for several key roles.
- *Role placements*: Once you have calculated the above metric, track it over the coming year to see if you actually fill open positions with the people who were identified on the succession plans. The

purpose of this measure is twofold: to assess the extent to which you can accurately predict who will be the future leaders and a check and balance on the first metric. As the first metric receives more attention, people will be tempted to pad their "ready now" lists with names to look good. By assessing if future leaders are actually drawn from the list, you guard against this tendency.

• *Succession plan effectiveness*: Assess the extent to which new leaders are successful in their positions after one year (e.g., they are still with the company and performing well). This metric also serves two purposes. First, it is a check and balance on the quality of people who were promoted; that is, people are less likely to throw unprepared leaders into new positions. Perhaps more importantly, this metric reinforces the importance of setting new leaders up for success.

Some of the best metrics to assess *organizational talent* include the following:

• *Recruitment and staffing*: One of the indicators of a strong organization is the extent to which you can attract good people into your organization, especially in jobs that are essential to your business objectives. Recruitment and staffing metrics might include the average time to fill key positions or job offer acceptance rates. When tracked by position, metrics like this have helped large organizations like Microsoft and Boeing identify talent gaps and target their recruiting efforts.

• *Performance management metrics*: If most development occurs on the job, the employee development and performance management systems are critical for employee development (see chapters 14 and 15). At the most basic level, measure if managers complete (1) performance goals, (2) development plans (if a separate process), and (3) end-of-year performance evaluations for themselves and people who work for them. You also might work with HR to assess the quality of the goals, development plans, and performance evaluations. There are other measures of employee engagement, but these three are the ones that provide the framework and foundation that everything else is built on.

• *Employee attrition (turnover) rates:* It is always a good idea to track the number and basic demographics (e.g., level, tenure, location, "regretted/nonregretted," gender, etc.) of people who leave the company. As noted below, one of the disadvantages is that this is a lagging indicator, only telling you that there is a problem. However, if problems are present, it is critical that you know about them!

While there are a variety of other leadership bench strength and talent management metrics (see Table 4.1)[1] we recommend starting with those suggested above for the following reasons:

1 They tend to counterbalance each other. For example, "cheating" on any one of the suggested metrics will negatively affect the others. For instance, padding leadership bench strength slates with weak candidates will mean that these candidates aren't likely to be chosen; and, if they are chosen, will be more likely to fail in their jobs in the first year. In the same way, time-to-hire metrics are important, but only tell part of the story. An organization also needs to assess if the people hired are successful in their jobs, are being developed, and stay with the company.
2 Holding people accountable for the above metrics is less likely to result in unanticipated negative consequences in the organization. For example, employee surveys can be great *diagnostic* indicators, but can be problematic *evaluative* measures. Both authors know of circumstances when managers, accountable in some manner for employee survey scores, have completed and submitted surveys for all their subordinates so as to be guaranteed high ratings for themselves. We have recommended metrics that will encourage behaviors that will improve organizational practices when they are addressed. For example, the best way to reduce turnover rates is to manage people better.
3 The suggested metrics are good "early warning systems" signaling managers to look deeper to see what is going on.

The talent management metrics that are most important in your organization will depend on your specific business strategy, the size and maturity of your organization, the talent pools that are most important to its success, and the data that are available. The following are some of the other issues you should consider.

Track Both "Process" and "Outcome" Metrics

Consider including both process and outcome talent management metrics. Organizations that only track the *outcome* measures don't know what to do when they find a problem. Organizations that only track the *process* metrics never know if they have achieved the results they want – a strong and talented workforce. Some important process metrics to monitor might include development plan completion rates, the quality of the development plans, and employee survey scores on items that are related to career development issues (e.g., "My manager and I have discussed my future career opportunities in the company"). Outcome metrics can vary from things like the succession effectiveness metric discussed earlier (e.g., the success of new leaders in the first year on the job), to true outcome measures (e.g., business performance, individual leader effectiveness, turnover rates).

Look for the Leading Indicators

The best metrics are the ones that indicate whether you have the talent that you need today *and* the talent you will need to meet future challenges. Unfortunately, the metrics that are easiest to obtain are often lagging indicators. High employee turnover, for example, only tells you that your talent has already walked out the door! The best diagnostic metrics are the ones that will proactively signal that something needs to be done before it's too late. Leadership bench strength measures, for example, when part of a rigorous succession management process, can highlight leadership gaps in the organization that will need to be addressed. Likewise, employee surveys can signal emerging issues in employee attitudes, especially when they are trended over time (e.g., Do managers and employees continue to say they see future career opportunities in the company? Do they continue to report that their jobs make good use of their skills and abilities?) This type of information can also be used to highlight specific business groups or employee groups where action is needed. For example, you might find that first-level manager survey scores are significantly lower than other management groups signaling a problem in this group that needs more attention.

This of course doesn't mean that lagging indicators should be ignored because they can provide valuable insights, especially when combined with leading indicators. For example, organizations can combine employee survey data with employee turnover data – using someone like an external consultant to protect employee confidentiality – to identify survey items that are predictive of later employee turnover. Using this type of analysis an organization might find that employees' satisfaction with their manager is the best predictor of whether people stay or not; while equally likely factors (e.g., pay, satisfaction with teammates, benefits) are less related to turnover. Combining indicators can begin to uncover some of these hidden relationships.

Link the Metrics to the Business Strategy

Business strategy can and should drive the talent metrics that are most relevant. Your ultimate goal is to choose the fewest metrics that will allow you to proactively understand whether you have the leaders and talent you need to achieve your organizational goals.[2] Some metrics will be better measures than others. For example, an organization that is expanding in Asia will probably want to pay particular attention to the leaders and talent in that region. Retail stores will focus special attention on store managers. As you think about your organization, what are the employee groups and talent management metrics that will most affect your success?

Don't Forget About Experience

We spent considerable time in the first chapter discussing how to identify the key experiences in your organization and how to assess the breadth and depth of these experiences at an individual level. When tracked at the organizational level, the data can be used to assess the combined experience of your leadership population. For example, you may find lots of leaders with start-up experience, but relatively few leaders who have turned around a failing business. This kind of data is especially powerful when combined with average leadership competency scores (see chapter 2) and average relationship scores (see chapter 3). Together, they can provide an important snapshot of leadership in the organization – the experiences, competencies, and relationships where leaders tend to be strong and areas where there are alarming gaps.

Organizations like Microsoft have used this kind of data to discover which experiences, competencies and relationships are most predictive of later leadership performance. When broken down by leadership level, it can be used to identify the key leadership "success factors" at each management level.[3] For example, managerial goal-setting skills might emerge as the most critical for first-level supervisors, networking skills for mid-level managers, and strategic thinking skills for senior leaders.

Taking Action

Look for Metrics that are Easily Available

Find the data that already exist in your organization. Many organizations have employee surveys that contain several items that capture how employees feel about their development. Performance management and development plan completion rates are usually available and easy to track. The HR department often has access to turnover rates by department, job type, or geographic location. Don't give up on creating the best metrics, but start with the data that you have right now.

Use Talent Management Metrics to Diagnose First, and Evaluate Second

There is truth in the wisdom that people only take something seriously if it is measured. Thus measuring leadership development will help demonstrate that it is a top priority for your organization. However, organizations need to be equally careful to avoid incentivizing the wrong behaviors. As you know, people can be extremely creative in finding ways to give you the numbers you want. For example, consider the typical succession management system. As indicated at the beginning of Part I, one of the best measures of an organization's leadership bench strength is the average number of internal leaders who are "ready now" to step into the position. At this point, several leaders will likely think to themselves, "So you want two 'ready now' successors for my job? Fine, I can give you two names." Are they good successors? Are they really ready now? Probably not. To avoid this kind of game-playing, some companies instead measure the average "time to fill" key leadership positions. Unfortunately, this strategy can also drive the wrong actions when

leaders decide to promote people who aren't ready yet, and the organization suffers the consequences for years to come.

Immediately evaluating leaders on metrics can lead them to start
"gaming" the system, focusing on how they can get the numbers
instead of using them to improve the organization. By introducing
them as a diagnostic tool first, you allow everybody to approach the
metrics as a way to learn what's working and what's not, and establish
some benchmarks for improvement. Then you can hold people
accountable to the action plans they have put in place to respond to
the numbers. Eventually, you may decide to use them for evaluation.
However, by using the metrics as diagnostic tools first, people are given
a chance to experiment with them. When managers are later held
accountable for improvements, they are more likely to be confident in
the validity of the ratings and their abilities to improve them.

There is an important caveat: Metrics that are designed explicitly
for development should never be used for evaluation. Let's take 360-
feedback ratings as an example. Research suggests that the ratings
tend to be inflated when they are used for evaluation.[4] Employees are
hesitant to rate their bosses poorly when they know that their boss
will be the person evaluating them at the end of the year. Clearly
specify up front whether the metric will be used for development or
for evaluation, and then vigorously ensure that the data are used only
in this way.

One More Time – Keep it Simple!

Trying to track too many metrics can be distracting, discouraging,
and ultimately, counterproductive. Only a *few* metrics are likely to
be the real drivers in your business. Even if you settle on two or three
metrics, be forewarned: They have the potential to get considerably
more complicated when you begin to take them seriously. Organizations can dedicate so much effort to data analysis that they never get
to the action stage. So keep the measures and the analysis as simple
as possible. The metrics are simply tools to assess how you are doing,
what needs to change, and the actions that will most effectively fix
the problem. Ask yourself, "What measures and level of analysis do
I need in order to take action on the results?" If you are like most
managers, you will *never* have enough information. Take a minute to
look over the list of metrics in Table 4.1 on pages 41–2. Then ask

yourself, "What are the 3–5 metrics that will *best* tell me if I have the leaders and talent in place to make this business successful?"

A Word of Warning – You Will Never Find the "Perfect" Metric

Every metric will come with its own set of strengths and weaknesses. Rather than give up, identify a short list of metrics and be clear about what they do and do not tell you. Establishing a set of talent management metrics is always better than trying to manage the organization with no information.

Table 4.1 Metrics to Watch

Talent management dimension	Metrics to watch
Succession management	**Leadership bench strength** • Key positions with at least two "ready now" candidates; and at least two "ready in one move" candidates • Time to fill key positions • Internal vs. external hires • Assessment of leaders against the experiences, competencies, and relationship taxonomies discussed in chapters 1–3 • Overall leadership trends (e.g., common strengths/weaknesses across all leaders, why leaders tend to derail) **Succession plan effectiveness** • Percentage of positions filled with people on the succession plan • Succession candidate success after one year • Movement between business units (if a corporate goal)
Employee development	**Employee survey scores** • Management support items • Career development items Development plans • Development plan completion rates • Development plan audits (see chapter 14) • Average employee tenure within jobs (measured against a target such as three years per job)

Table 4.1 Metrics to Watch *Continued*

Talent management dimension	Metrics to watch
	Leadership and employee capabilities • 360-feedback scores – overall, by business group, by management level, etc. • Mandatory training completion rates (e.g., skills certifications, EEO training, fair business practices training, etc.)
Performance management	**Performance goal effectiveness** • Performance goal on-time completion rates • Performance goal quality audit (e.g., specific goals, linked to business strategy, with metrics, etc.) **Performance appraisal effectiveness** • On-time completion rate • Performance appraisal quality audit (e.g., quality of comments by employee and manager) • Performance rating distributions
Employee engagement	**Recruitment and staffing** • Job offer acceptance rates • Tim to fill key positions • Success in job after 1 year **Employee survey items (in the following areas)** • Management support • Good use of skills, abilities, and strengths • Motivation (e.g., clear goals, accountability, feedback) • Employee satisfaction • Intention to stay **Retention (attrition)** • Overall turnover rates • Turnover rates during the first year • Turnover rates for key talent pools (e.g., leaders, engineers, IT) • Turnover rates by performance rating (to see if high performers are leaving at higher rates) **Other metrics** • Absenteeism rates • Grievance rates • Safety rates • Ethics violations

To Learn More

Becker, B. E., Huselid, M. A., & Ulrich, D. (2001). *The HR scorecard: Linking people, strategy and performance.* Boston, MA: Harvard Business School Press.

Corporate Leadership Council. (2005). *The metrics standard: Establishing standards for 200 core human capital measures.* Washington, DC: Corporate Executive Board.

Fitz-enz, J., & Davison, B. (2002). *How to measure human resources management* (3rd ed.). New York: McGraw Hill.

Ittner, C. D., & Larcker, D. F. (2003). Coming up short: On nonfinancial performance measurement. *Harvard Business Review,* **81**(11), 88–95.

Silzer, R., & Dowell, B. (in press). *Strategy driven talent management: A leadership imperative.* San Francisco, CA: Jossey-Bass.

Part II

Capturing the Lessons

In Part I, we discussed the ways you can identify the leadership experiences, competencies, and relationships that are most important in your organization. In Part II, we discuss how you can get the most out of those experiences. Learning from experience doesn't happen by chance. It requires the courage to step into the unknown, the insight to choose the right stretch assignments, the skills to navigate through them successfully, the ability to capture the lessons, and the capacity to correct your course when you find yourself derailing.

Chapter 5 focuses on the factors that will allow you to take the career risks that are necessary for your development. Make no mistake, leadership is risky. There is no guarantee you will succeed. Unfortunately, the only way you will know the limits of your leadership potential is to put yourself into these "edge of your comfort zone" experiences.

Chapter 6 focuses on the critical elements that you should build into a stretch assignment. Some positions, no matter how good they look on paper, just aren't developmental. Fortunately, research in I-O psychology has identified a range of elements that can turn a job into a powerful developmental experience.

Chapter 7 focuses on what you can do to navigate through the assignments and emerge a better leader on the other side. This chapter discusses practical ideas you can use to navigate successfully through challenging experiences.

Chapter 8 is devoted to how you can reflect on, capture, and apply the lessons you are learning. The focus of this chapter is on "real time reflection"; that is, the kind of reflection that you can integrate directly into your leadership activities and do in the moment. Real time reflection allows you to execute the business strategy in such a way that you are improving and developing as you go.

Chapter 9 focuses on what you can do when you find yourself derailed, off-course, or plateaued in your career. We discuss the common causes of derailment, the warning signs, and the strategies you can use to get back on track.

Chapter 5

Stepping into the Unknown

The Challenge

If most development occurs in trial-by-fire experiences, then obviously you should throw yourself into these types of situations. That sounds like great advice – for someone else! Doing this to yourself might seem, well, a little masochistic. Yet leaders do this all the time. So what allows leaders to step into the unknown? In our work with managers, several themes consistently emerged that allowed leaders to step into stretch assignments that were right at the edge of their comfort zones.

First, let's define what we mean by the "edge of your comfort zone." This is a place where you are confident you are good enough, but the job will really stretch you in new areas. For example, CitiCorp tries to place high-potential managers in jobs for which they are 60–70 percent prepared.[1] You have the basics but will have to develop new skills to excel. The leaders we spoke to describe these kinds of experiences as places where they felt excited and fearful at exactly the same time.

Leaders who were willing to step into these places talked about a job where they had the chance to stretch and grow. They were in a place where they could make a difference. They had a great network of people to support them. Some leaders admitted that they were motivated by less noble-sounding reasons. Some took stretch jobs because of the increased status that came with them. Others just couldn't pass up the pay. In a few cases, leaders didn't know what they were really getting into until it was too late!

In this chapter, we will focus our discussion on the actionable strategies that allow leaders to step to the edge of themselves.

The Bottom Line

Reframe the Edge as a Possibility, Not a Problem

Ultimately, going to the edge is the only way to develop, test, and refine the breadth and depth of your leadership capabilities and expand your capacity. Moving to the edge starts with your potential and your strengths, not your weaknesses.[2] This doesn't mean that you ignore weaknesses. Ignoring your weaknesses is one of the surest paths to derailment (see chapter 9). Likewise, we aren't suggesting that you should focus only on the positive. Research suggests that overreliance on one's strengths and "what's always worked for me before" are also common paths to derailment and failure.[3] Focusing on potential means starting with your strengths and considering your weaknesses second, in the context of possibility.[4]

Take a moment to test yourself. Consider the challenges that you face right now in your business and personal development. Do you focus first on the possibilities or the problems? Do you think of challenges as problems to overcome or as a way to expand your leadership capacity? Is your development plan built around "gaps" and areas where you are weak or focused on your future direction, considering the full range of skills that will be needed (including expanding on some strengths, developing new capabilities in untested areas, and addressing gaps)? Now, consider your direct reports. In the last development conversations that you had with them, did you spend more time talking about their strengths or their weaknesses? Do their development plans focus as much attention on developing their strengths as they do to overcoming their weaknesses?

Look for Assignments that Take You to Your Edge

Look for assignments where you aren't too comfortable, *and* where you don't feel out of control. If you're too comfortable you are likely to rely on the way you have always done it. You won't have the opportunity or need to develop new skills. On the other hand, if you are too far outside your comfort zone, you are probably too stressed to capture the lessons and make them a part of your repertoire. The brain doesn't retain much information when it is stressed. The most developmental assignments will tend to be the ones where you are confident you can do the job (e.g., your strengths will get you through), but you will be stretched in other areas to expand your skills, experiment in untested areas, and overcome weaknesses. From an emotional standpoint, look for the jobs that you approach with both excitement and fear.

Find Your Purpose

When we have talked with leaders about the times they stepped into the unknown and took on assignments that were at the edge of their comfort zones, many leaders talked about the challenge in the context of a larger personal mission. They talked about taking on jobs because they could accomplish work that was bigger than themselves. They had a sense of purpose that transcended the challenges they were facing. For example, this might be a leader who agrees to take over an organization that is failing and needs to be downsized by 50 percent, because the leader is confident that the business can be saved, and that he or she can make the right decisions with compassion.[5]

Focus on the Learning

Recent research in psychology suggests that people do best when they have a learning – rather than a performance – orientation.[6] People with a learning orientation are more likely to take on new challenges because they believe that they can learn as they go. They focus on iterative learning cycles, and getting better over time. In contrast, people who primarily focus on performance tend to do well and remain motivated until they fail. Then they are more likely to define the failure as a reflection on their inherent ability (e.g., "I'm just not talented or smart enough to do this well"). Leaders who focus on learning, however, are more likely to look for lessons they can learn and actions they can do differently in the next challenge (e.g., "What did I learn?"). Learning-oriented people aren't any less driven, but consider their leadership development as an iterative process and always ask themselves how they can be different and better leaders a year from now. Take a few minutes and consider your current job. Are you trying to perform at 100 percent all of the time, or are you focused on learning as you go and building a body of accomplishments over the life of your career?

Focus on What You Can Control

A leader's perspective going into a tough situation can make all the difference in whether or not he or she chooses to take on the next big challenge. Leaders who step into the unknown and navigate successfully through those times have an internal locus of control. They realistically acknowledge the things that aren't in their control, but then step back to focus their attention and energy on the things they can influence. They take time to "step onto the balcony,"[7] focus on the big picture, and find the places in the larger system where their efforts can make a difference.

Draw on Others

Part III discusses the critical role that other people play in the development of leaders. The people in your network are the ones who can open possibilities, stretch your thinking, and provide support when needed. Role models, mentors, bosses, and other people in your life often provide the impetus and boost your confidence to take on the next stretch assignment. Role models provide the vision and possibility. Mentors and bosses can sometimes have more confidence in you than you have in yourself. They are the ones who provide the insight, support, feedback, and encouragement to navigate through the unknown. It's important to identify the people who can be most helpful in these situations. Look for the ones who can be brutally honest with you and yet, after the conversation, somehow leave you feeling more energized than you were before.

Expand Your Career Agility

The leaders most willing to take chances are the ones who have several career possibilities; that is, they are less dependent on their current jobs. They have skill sets that are transferable, and strong external networks. This gives them the freedom to say what needs to be said and do what needs to done in their current role because they aren't crippled with a fear of losing their job. They are confident they have the skills to make significant and regular job changes in their careers, if needed. The bottom line is that they can take more career risks because they have other options.

Taking Action

Where is Your Edge?

Where can you stretch and challenge yourself? What projects can you take on where you are confident your strengths will ensure that you are "good enough," but you will be stretched in new areas? What hidden talents and possibilities will have the chance to emerge if you put yourself in this kind of stretch assignment?

Assess Your Strategies

Consider an area in your current job where you are at your edge. Assess yourself against the dimensions listed in the box below. Find the strategies that you rely on the most and consider how you can leverage them even more. Consider strategies that you tend to ignore and consider how you can better use them in the future.

Challenge Your Team

Encourage your team members to identify how they want to push themselves to their edge. Together identify some projects and challenges in their current jobs that will challenge them to grow and develop. Adopt a potential focus, communicate confidence that you believe they are up to the task, and challenge them to develop themselves in untested areas. Ask them to make use of the strategies outlined in the box above and discuss outcomes during a team meeting. Consider the kind of leader you are for your team. Do you focus on problems or potential? Do they believe you are committed to their success? Can you be honest with your team, giving them hard feedback, but do it in a way that focuses on their potential? Are people more energized after talking to you?

Strategies for Stepping into the Unknown

Consider an area in your current job where you feel stretched. Look over the list below and rate how much you are relying on each of the dimensions. If you aren't currently stretched, consider another area of your life where you feel stretched or a previous job where you found yourself at the edge of your comfort zone. Rate each dimension on a five-point scale from (1) *Not used*, to (5) *Frequently used*. When you are done, go back over the list and consider how you can leverage the dimensions where you are strong to take on future challenges. Use the reflection questions to consider the dimensions you tend to overlook.

Rating	Dimension	Reflection
	Focus on potential: the extent to which you have framed the challenge as the way to discover your potential, identify unrealized strengths, and refine your skills.	• Where is your leadership edge – the place where you feel excitement and fear at exactly the same time? • What future job assignment would best put you at the edge of your comfort zone; the place where you are confident you can be "good enough" but you would be stretched in areas where you want to develop?
	Find your purpose: the extent to which you have a sense of purpose that transcends the challenges that you are facing right now.	• What is the legacy that you want to leave in your current job? • What do you want your team to remember about you? • What would you do if you weren't afraid?
	Focus on the learning: the extent to which you are motivated to learn and grow, to see learning as a process, and are focused on increasing your competence over time (versus focusing all of your attention on performing well, gaining favorable judgments from others, and avoiding negative judgments about your competence).	• What are your top three development goals in your current assignment? • How do you hope you will be a different leader on the other side of this assignment? • What are some strategies you can put in place to learn from mistakes and adjust your course as you go along? • Rather than focus on performing at 100% all of the time, what is the body of accomplishments you would like to leave over the life of your career?

	Focus on what you can control: the extent to which you stay focused on what you can control and influence rather than focusing on the things that are out of your control.	• What are the top three priorities in your job? • What is in your control? What can you influence? What do you need to let go?
	Draw on others: the extent to which you have available, and actively draw on, a broad network of people for encouragement, coaching, feedback, and advice.	• Who are two people in your life you can rely on for emotional support and use as sounding boards? • Who can give you tough advice and energize you at the same time? • Who has been through a similar challenge before and can serve as a mentor and advisor to you? • Who are three people in your current network you can draw on to make up for your weaknesses?
	Expand your career agility: the extent to which you are confident that you have control over your career, have a range of career options available to you, and can successfully manage through the challenges that you face.	• In your field, what are the skills that are most valuable and most transferable? • When you have struggled in the past, what has gotten you through? • What are three jobs, inside or outside your current company, that you could take tomorrow? • If you lost your job today, who are three people you could call? When is the last time you talked with them?

Lead Your Organization into the Unknown

Think about the business challenges your organization is facing. How can you use the dimensions discussed in this chapter to effectively lead your organization into the unknown? What actions, messages, and processes can you put into place to build these dimensions into your organization? What messages will be most relevant and motivating to the people in your organization?

To Learn More

Block, P. (2002). *The answer to how is yes.* San Francisco, CA: Barrett-Koehler.

Heifitz, R. A., & Linsky, M. (2002). A survival guide for leaders. *Harvard Business Review,* **80(6)**, 65–74.

McKenna, R. B., & Yost, P. R. (2004). The differentiated leader: Specific strategies for handling today's adverse situations. *Organizational Dynamics,* **33**, 292–306.

Whyte, D. (2001). *Crossing the unknown sea: Work as a pilgrimage of identity.* New York: Riverhead Books.

Chapter 6

Stretch Assignments

The Challenge

Think back to the greatest development experiences in your career. Chances are you simply found yourself in the right place at the right time. In other words, you got lucky. And if it was a great experience, you probably can identify in retrospect what made it so powerful. However, at the time, you probably were just trying to survive! What if you could identify in advance the ingredients that make up a great development assignment so you can proactively seek them out?

In this chapter we discuss in more detail the essential elements of stretch assignments and offer practical actions for increasing the amount of stretch – not stress – in your current role. We also discuss how you can use this information to build systems that will help leaders throughout your organization challenge, stretch, and grow their leadership capabilities.

The Bottom Line

Stretch is All About the Mismatch

The jobs with the most development potential will be the ones that present new experiences, challenges, and relationships that the leader hasn't faced before (see chapters 1–3). Development, then, is a matter of identifying and putting yourself into assignments that will expose you to these new areas. This might be a new role or taking on a project that challenges you to develop in new ways. To develop your team in place, look for ways that they can share or trade assignments to stretch themselves and develop new skills.

Some organizations only look for stretch assignments for the people they have identified as "high potential" leaders. But if stretch assignments are really any assignments where leaders' current experiences, competencies, and skills don't match the job, it means that almost any assignment can be a stretch assignment for the right person. Of course, there will always be a limited number of senior leadership roles and a limited number of assignments in any given business group, but if you look broadly across the organization, there are likely to be an abundance of opportunities that will challenge individuals to stretch and grow their capabilities.

Make Sure it Really is a Stretch Assignment

The best assignment on paper can be a waste of time in reality. Several key elements are necessary for an assignment to be truly developmental.[1] Stretch assignments require leaders to use new skills, or old skills at significantly more sophisticated levels. They require leaders to take the organization or their departments in a new direction and get things done through other people. The best stretch assignments include lots of feedback sources, from the work itself and from other people. Support systems are also important, and might include a network of people inside and outside of the organization, a manager with high expectations and confidence in the leader, and/or a strong team that reports to the leader. The "How to Build a Stretch Assignment" box below provides a more comprehensive list of these elements. In addition, the *Job Challenge Profile* is a commercially available research-based assessment that leaders can use to quantitatively assess the developmental potential of their jobs.[2]

Be Intentional About the Assignments You Chose

Development shouldn't be thought of as something that is added to the job. It should happen while leaders are doing the job. Strategic stretch assignments are the ones that "kill two birds with one stone" – requiring leaders to execute the business strategy and develop their leadership capabilities along the way. Unfortunately, many aspiring leaders aren't intentional about the assignments they accept and are forced to add developmental activities on top of their regular daily responsibilities. In this way, it's not development first, but development in the service of performance. Leaders will still need to be intentional about how they expect to grow in the assignment, but the activities used to get there can be a natural part of their daily work.

Taking Action

Stretch Yourself

Consider your current job. Are you in one of the key experiences that you identified in chapter 1? To be successful in your current role, do you need to develop and use some of the leadership competencies that you identified in chapter 2? Does the job require you to develop some of the relationships you identified in chapter 3? What are some projects and assignments on the horizon that would offer these kinds of challenges? Now review the box below to see if your current job contains the elements that will make it a true stretch assignment. Looking over the list, identify elements you can add to your job to make it a more powerful developmental experience. Remember, your goal is to find or create an assignment that will develop you without adding a lot of extra work. Imagine a job where your performance goals are your development goals!

Stretch Your Team

As the leader, you have a great opportunity to think strategically about the development of your team. Consider how you can use assignments to develop the people on your team. If they are leaders, challenge them to rate themselves on the experiences, competencies, and relationships that you mapped out in the earlier chapters, and identify areas where they would like to develop. Consider opportunities for your direct reports to swap job responsibilities. Challenge them to find ways to use the elements in the box above to increase the stretch in their current jobs.

Build a Stretch Organization

Senior business and HR leaders also need to consider larger systemic issues. They need to create an organization where stretch assignments are a natural part of the culture, where the HR systems support

Tips:
How to Build a Stretch Assignment

Take a few moments and consider your current job. Use this list to identify ways that you can increase the stretch and developmental potential of your job or the jobs of the people who report to you. For leaders who are feeling overly stretched, focus special attention on the support elements at the end of the list.

New Directions and Experiences

☐ I will lead my team through significant changes in the coming year.
☐ I inherited problems in this job that will need to be overcome.
☐ Excellence is clearly defined in this job.
☐ I will be exposed to the critical experiences, competencies, and relationships that I identified at the beginning of this book.

Running the Business

☐ The work of my team will significantly impact the success of the organization.
☐ The job requires me to work closely with senior leaders and/or the board of directors of the organization.
☐ In this job, I feel I need to deliver value daily.
☐ My successes or failures are highly visible in this job assignment.

Getting Things Done Through Others

☐ I have to influence people and groups over whom I have no formal authority.
☐ I am the one who will be held responsible if the team doesn't accomplish its goals.
☐ I have to work in partnership with multiple stakeholders who have contradictory and competing agendas.
☐ I'm not an expert in the work that I have to manage.
☐ I am responsible for a diverse group of businesses, functions, and/or people.
☐ I have to work with difficult people to get things done.

New Leadership Skills

☐ This job pushes me to the edge of my comfort zone.

☐ This job presents significant challenges that I've never faced before in areas that I consider important for my development.

☐ The job will be a big transition from anything I have experienced before.

☐ This job will require me to significantly expand my leadership capabilities (i.e., overcoming weaknesses, developing my strengths, or developing new skills in previously untested areas).

☐ I don't have enough time to accomplish everything I want to accomplish, forcing me to make tough leadership choices and to get things done through other people.

Feedback

☐ Clear metrics and ongoing feedback are available.

☐ Feedback is frequent, immediate, specific, and tells me how I'm doing against my goals for the year.

☐ I get open and sometimes painfully honest feedback from others on how I'm doing.

☐ I reflect on the business and my development as a leader.

Support

☐ I have to work closely with suppliers, partners, customers, or other external stakeholders that are critical to the organization's success.

☐ My manager has set high expectations for me and is confident that I can reach them.

☐ I lead a strong and talented team that is committed to excellence.

☐ I have a strong network of people that I can draw on inside and outside the company who can provide support, advice, and coaching.

stretch assignments, and where talent management metrics are tracked to ensure people are being developed.

Stretch organizations start with a stretch culture. This is a culture where employees assume the world is changing, and standing still means falling behind. There is the expectation that employees will take on new challenges every two to three years – either in their current positions or in a new assignment. In a large company, leaders are willing and expected to move between organizations. Lateral moves are valued. Managers, peers, and employees are willing to give each other candid feedback. Employees look for new trends that are emerging in the industry and in their field of expertise. They know the company strategy and seek out jobs that will lead to the development of increasingly important skill sets.

Leaders play an important role in creating this type of culture. They can discuss external trends that will impact the business. They can be role models by taking on new challenges themselves, talking about the struggles and challenges they face, and identifying the strategies they are using to navigate through them. They can encourage the members of their leadership teams to take on new assignments and hold them accountable for doing the same with the employees they have responsibility for.

The HR systems can often be the greatest barriers to cultural change, but they can also be instrumental in catalyzing and supporting the change. Organizations that put a premium on employee development are more likely to ensure that all employees complete development plans every year, and hold managers accountable for discussing them with employees. They have rigorous performance management processes in place. They encourage employees to take on new assignments with a transparent and efficient internal job posting system. They ensure that senior leaders are moving between business units and implement an effective succession management process to fill senior roles.

Stretch organizations also monitor and track how well they are doing in each of these areas. They track how long people tend to stay in jobs. They use employee surveys to measure more than just employee satisfaction, but also to measure the extent to which employees feel that they are being stretched and developed. What gets measured gets done. See chapter 4 for some measures that can be used to assess these talent management dimensions.

To Learn More

For further discussions about the key elements of stretch assignments, see:

Lombardo, M. M., & Eichinger, R. W. (1988). *Eighty-eight assignments for development in place.* Greensboro, NC: Center for Creative Leadership.

McCauley, C. D. (2006). *Developmental assignments: Creating learning experiences without changing jobs.* Greensboro, NC: Center for Creative Leadership.

McCall, M. W. (1998). *High flyers: Developing the next generation of leaders.* Boston, MA: Harvard Business School Press.

Simons, R. (2005). Designing high-performance jobs. *Harvard Business Review,* **83(7/8)**, 54–62.

Chapter 7

Navigating the Experiences

The Challenge

Finding the right stretch assignments and having the courage to take them are the first two steps to personal leadership development, but they aren't enough. You also need to be able to successfully navigate through the assignments. You need to make sure you are doing the things that will allow you to emerge a better leader on the other side.

In this chapter, we will discuss some simple strategies you can employ to maximize your learning in the experience. The focus here is on *simple* because leaders always have too much to do. Business performance can always be improved. Processes can always be streamlined. People can always be developed. Adding a bunch of "developmental activities" on top of these goals can be overwhelming, so one of the secrets of continuous development is to build a supportive environment and adopt habits that enable your personal growth *in the midst* of daily challenges. Most of these habits fall under the broad umbrella that is known in psychology as "self-management." They are based on decades of research on how people manage themselves and their learning. A more academic discussion can be found elsewhere.[1] Here we focus on the practical application of the research.

The Bottom Line

Manage Your Learning

Leaders don't develop by accident. They have to work at it. Scientists have devoted their energies for several decades to understanding what motivates and drives people to do what they do and how people can manage and change behaviors. Research findings suggest there are several strategies that leaders can use to manage themselves more effectively. Among the most important are: setting goals, creating and managing cues, monitoring your progress, analyzing barriers and supports, creating personal accountability, and identifying rewards and punishments.[2] Reflection is also important – so important, in fact, that we have devoted the entire next chapter to the subject. Below are some examples of how each of these strategies can be used to support your development as a leader.

Goals. Clearly *defining* your goals and *committing* yourself to them are the first two steps to effective self-management. But all goals are not equal. Some kinds of goals will consistently lead to improvement and other goals will consistently lead to ... well, to be honest ... nothing. In the hundreds of studies that have been done in this area, the results are astonishingly consistent:[3] People who set goals that are specific and difficult yet attainable outperform people who have "do your best" or easy goals. In complex environments – like the ones leaders face every day – you will need to make choices between competing priorities. You should set *both* long-term career goals and clear, short-term development goals that lead to your long-term objectives. Visualize the kind of leader you want to be when you have improved. How will your leadership be different? What will people say about you? Remember that there will be lots of ups and downs in your journey to get there. How will you stay focused when you are struggling and how will you pick yourself up along the way?

Cues. Cues are the reminders that trigger the desired behavior. They are what keep you focused. Let's take an example: If you were trying to lose weight, you could post your goal on the refrigerator, remove all unhealthy food from your house and replace it with healthy food, and put your exercise gear by the door every night. In the same way, consider the reminders that you could use to keep your development goals in front of you. For example, consider something as simple as posting your development goals somewhere in your office where you can see them. Or schedule time once a month on your calendar to review your performance *and* your development goals. Removing negative cues is equally important. For example, consider reviewing your performance and development goals *before* you check your email in the morning so you are less likely to be distracted by the crises of the day.

Self-monitoring. Self-monitoring simply means tracking how you are doing. This doesn't have to be a formal or complicated tracking system; rather, it is making the time weekly to ask yourself questions such as: Where am I spending most of my time these days? When am I at my best? When am I at my worst? What am I learning? However, just answering these questions sometimes isn't enough, and you will want to use some simple techniques to numerically track how you are doing. For example, let's say your goal is to increase the amount of coaching that you provide to your team. You could track the amount of time you spend in one-on-one conversations with your direct reports every day or the time you spend in development conversations with them each week. Or consider a more tactical approach – for example, put three coins in your left pocket and move one to your right pocket every time you coach someone instead of telling them the answer.

Barriers and support. To make any significant change, it is important to identify what factors will help or hinder your efforts to change. Emerging research suggests that people are significantly more likely to change their behavior when they identify barriers and proactively plan how they are going to respond.[4] For any behavior you are trying to change, ask yourself: What consistently gets in the way of the change? What will I do the next time I encounter this barrier? What can I put in place and who can I draw on to help support this change?

Accountability. Asking other people to hold you accountable to your development goals raises the stakes. Accountability can be as simple as telling your manager, peers, or your direct reports about your goals, and asking them how you are doing. Scheduling time to pro-actively seek their feedback is even better.

Rewards and punishment. The rule is simple – people will tend to do what gets rewarded and avoid what gets punished. However, the real world gets a little more complicated. In a complex environment, choosing some activities means other activities won't get done. Committing to an exercise program could mean less sleep or less time with your family. Understanding the real reinforcers in your environment means asking yourself the following questions: What is in it for me if I pursue my goals? What is the pay-off if I don't change? What will I have to give up if I spend time on my development? How can I change the rewards and punishments so the environment is more closely aligned with my priorities?

Build a Supportive Environment

It's great for individuals to be motivated and engaged and open to learning but it is equally important that the culture of the organization values learning. In order to build and maintain this kind of culture, three factors are particularly important: (1) management support, (2) candid feedback, and (3) an effective reward system.[5]

Management support: The words and actions of senior leaders signal what is valued. It's important that they signal that development and performance are both important. But it's not only top management that shapes the environment. Managers at all levels have an enormous impact on the development of their direct reports. *You* have a powerful impact on the development of *your* direct reports! (See chapter 14 for a discussion of the important role that you play.)

Candid feedback: As noted earlier, development goals are relatively worthless without feedback. A feedback-rich environment is one where people are held accountable for their performance, and given frank and candid feedback about how they are doing, how they are being perceived, and what is needed in the future. Chapter 10 discusses the characteristics of effective feedback in more detail. Without feedback, it's just too easy for people to fool themselves. It's like the boy who shoots his arrow at the wall and then paints the bulls-eye around it, congratulating himself with "Another perfect shot!"

Effective reward systems: High performance organizations reward *both* performance and development. Employees are encouraged to take on new challenges and stretch themselves. The leaders who are recognized and promoted have a reputation for developing other people. Succession management systems and promotional decisions consider both how well leaders will perform in potential new assignments and how developmental it will be for them. Think about your organization. What supports (or gets in the way) of development?

Taking Action

Manage Yourself

Write out your development goals for the year, even if your organization doesn't require it. Use the motivation strategies discussed in the chapter to track your progress, identify what is holding you back, and create the conditions that will accelerate your growth. See the case scenario below.

Teach Your Team "How to Fish"

"Give a man a fish and he will eat for a day, but teach a man to fish and he will eat for the rest of his life," declares the Chinese proverb. As you work with your team, your job as their manager is not to teach them everything they need to know to do their job. Getting compliance is easy; getting commitment and growth is tough. In other words, the real challenge for your team isn't following your instructions; it's figuring out how to solve problems without you (and better than you). Your goal is to be the kind of leader that helps your team "learn how to learn." So your first job is to build a team that can perform at the highest level, but never lose sight of your second job: to develop a team of people who learn and grow on their own, constantly addressing new challenges and growing in ways that could not have been prescribed or even imagined.

Build Success into Your Organization

Ultimately, your job is to create an organization where people manage themselves in alignment with organizational goals. Your goal is what

Case Scenario:
Strategies for Learning from Experience

The Situation

Bob is a manager who gets results. He is driven and has a strong track record of success. He was recognized early in his career for his ability to get things done and his technical expertise. He is a high achiever and hates to lose. He drives his team equally hard. He sets high goals for himself and expects the same of his people – though never more than he asks of himself – and always challenges them to stretch themselves. Recently he got a promotion and realized that his strategy doesn't work in his new environment. He can't hold everyone personally accountable, but needs to develop systems that drive accountability throughout the organization. He also recognizes that he is the person driving the team and responsible for its energy, but he isn't building a team that can sustain itself. In meetings, people continue to look to him for "the answer" and the final decision. He suspects that he has created this situation. He wants to create a team that will succeed long after he is gone.

Self-Management Strategies

To change this situation, Bob might consider the following self-management strategies to start moving his leadership to the next level.

Goal setting: Bob moves beyond just setting organizational performance goals. He adds a goal to develop future leaders in his team, which helps him to focus his energy on driving change *through other people*. He also adds two development goals. The first is, "In the next 12 months, I will develop at least one leader who will be ready to step into my role and at least two more leaders who will be ready the following year." His second goal is, "Within one year, this organization can run without me." The achievement of these goals will free him up to focus more attention on the strategic issues that he doesn't have time to pursue today.

Barriers and support: Bob knows one-on-one meetings with team members are the place where he most often fails. He starts every meeting thinking of himself as a joint problem solver, but somewhere during the conversation he always seems to take over by coming up with "the" answer. He makes a commitment to himself that in the coming weeks he will only allow himself to identify outcomes, boundary conditions, and feedback sources, but the team member will be responsible for identifying the project plan, the milestones, and how the objectives will be achieved. Bob also commits to end every meeting with a date when the person will return with a plan. He imagines who will be most resistant to this new approach, and how he will respond. For example, Bob won't meet with one of his team members, Chris, who isn't very proactive in his work, if Chris doesn't come prepared or hasn't thought through his approach. Instead Bob will schedule a new meeting in the coming week when Chris will have a plan in hand. Bob also identifies situations that support his goals. He realizes that he is at his best if he takes 15 minutes to think about his goals and prepare for these meetings. It is when he feels rushed that he starts trying to solve the problems himself. He schedules 15 minutes before every meeting on his calendar.

Cues: Bob types up a standard agenda for his one-on-one meetings that he can use to keep himself honest. The agenda requires him to identify the goal of the meeting, what will be discussed, what the team member is responsible for, a set of questions he can ask to draw the other person out, and the outcomes he expects at the end of the meeting. Bob creates a similar outline for his staff meetings to help prevent him from taking over in these group discussions. He also uses red sticky dots as subtle reminders to ask questions and avoid playing the expert (e.g., he puts one on his phone as a reminder to empower and develop the leadership potential in the person calling).

Self-monitoring: Bob decides that one of the best ways to assess how much progress he is making is to track how many comments he makes in his weekly staff meetings. He decides to make a tally mark every time he gives advice in a meeting as a way to assess if he is playing the expert or helping to develop future leaders. He starts to notice how many of these comments he can actually turn into questions. He also notices that if he's quiet long enough, people start talking and helping each other. He finds it's a great way to assess how well he's doing over time.

Accountability: Bob shares his goals with his direct reports and his manager. He asks them to help hold him accountable. He makes a point every week of asking at least one of them, "How did I do?"

Rewards: Bob rewards himself for really good meetings by inviting one of his direct reports to coffee (which also serves as a great way to get to know them better). Ultimately the team is functioning at a higher level from both a performance and employee engagement perspective, making a real difference in the bottom line.

the Chinese philosopher Lao-Tzu wrote over 2,000 years ago: "Of the best leaders, when their work is done, the people will say, 'We did it ourselves.'" To really stretch yourself, consider the question: What can you do today that will have an impact on the business 10 years from now? The question requires you to move to systems-level thinking, considering the processes and practices you can put in place to meet challenges that you can't even anticipate. Execution isn't enough. Learning isn't enough. Building an organization that executes, learns, and improves with every cycle is the only option. Consider how you can build the self-management principles discussed in this chapter into the way your organization does business.

To Learn More

Drucker, P. F. (1999). Managing oneself. *Harvard Business Review*, **77**(2), 64–74.

Manz, C. C., & Sims, H. P. (1991). *The new superleadership: Leading others to lead themselves.* San Francisco, CA: Berrett-Koehler Publishers.

McCauley, C. D., Moxley, R. S., & Van Velsor, E. (2004). *The Center for Creative Leadership handbook of leadership development.* San Francisco, CA: Jossey-Bass.

Peterson, D. B., & Hicks, M. D. (1996). *Leader as coach: Strategies for coaching and developing others.* Minneapolis, MN: Personnel Decisions International.

Chapter 8

Real Time Reflection

The Challenge

After reading the title for this chapter, you may be thinking, "Reflection is a lovely idea, but I have a business to run!" Unfortunately, organizations today are often trying to run so fast that they seem to specialize in lessons *observed*, rather than lessons *learned*. The good news is that reflection doesn't have to take a lot of time and it can be done as a natural part of the business cycle. In this chapter, we will focus on what Kent Seibert calls "reflection-in-action" and we're calling *real time reflection*.[1] We'll discuss the kind of reflection that you can do in the moment, making it a natural part of your daily activities as you are pursuing your business goals. We'll also suggest some practices that you can put in place to help your team capture learning, and the actions you can take to build reflection into your organization so it is a natural part of everybody's job.

The Bottom Line

Be Intentional

One of the keys to real time reflection is to intentionally design reflection into your work. For example, as you review your calendar and priorities for the day, identify opportunities to practice the skills you want to develop. Take time at the end of the day to reflect on what you learned, to identify unexpected successes and failures, and think about any patterns that emerge in how you are leading. Use the questions in the "Daily Reflection" box to reflect on your day. Don't feel that you have to reflect on all the questions, but use them as catalysts to ensure you aren't just "doing" but also learning along the way.

Tips:
Daily Reflection

In the Morning

- Given my performance and development goals for the year, what are my highest priorities today?
- Considering my development goals, what is one thing I can practice today?

At the End of the Day

- What went well? What didn't work? Why?
- Looking back on my day, how closely did my actual results match what I expected? What were my unexpected successes? What were my unexpected failures? Are there any underlying patterns?
- How can I apply what I learned today to my work tomorrow?

Look for Learning Opportunities

Look for ways in which you can make learning a natural part of the job. Use daily problems to engage in what Chris Argyris, Professor Emeritus at Harvard Business School, has called double-loop learning; that is, not only solving the immediate problem, but figuring out how you can approach future problems more effectively.[2] For example, as you face business problems, consider how you can develop solutions that will generalize to other situations. Examine problems from multiple perspectives. Think about all the people whom the problem affects and consider how you can create a solution that works across multiple domains.

Identify your personal barriers to learning. What tends to get in your way? For example, do you get so caught up in your own thinking that you don't draw on other people? Or perhaps you get so consumed with making sure everyone is heard or in exploring all possibilities that you don't drive action. Do you tend to overthink decisions or make decisions too quickly? Consider how you learn best: through reading, listening to other people, or working the problem out through action. How can you best leverage this method? What methods do you tend to overlook? Develop a short list of questions that you can ask yourself when you face new challenges. The key is to make sure that you use business problems as the raw material to strengthen your thinking skills and to develop yourself!

Don't Forget Deeper Reflection

Just as good business strategy includes both short-term and long-term planning, your personal development requires that you build in opportunities for both short-term and long-term reflection. Long-term reflection doesn't require a two-week retreat in the mountains. It may be a block of several hours you consciously set aside to consider what you have learned over the past 12 months, to reflect on any trends and patterns that you are seeing, and to think about your long-term development. How did you do against the development goals you set for yourself? When were you at your best? When were you at your worst? When did you struggle? When did you learn the most (e.g., in what situations and from whom)? What was different about these times? How are you a different leader today than you were a year ago? Looking forward, where do you want to be in three years? In 10 years? Based on your answers, what should be your development goals in the coming year?

Taking Action

Keep it Simple

Find ways to make reflection a natural part of your day. As you plan your day, look for a time when you can practice at least one of your developmental goals. Build milestones into your projects to analyze what is working well, what isn't working, and what you want to improve going forward. Put a sticky note in your car reminding you to reflect on your day: to celebrate successes and find at least one lesson learned. At the end of the week, ask yourself, "What did I learn and how can I apply those lessons in the coming week?"

Draw on Others

Find another leader and meet for lunch monthly to discuss the struggles you are facing and what you are learning. Put yourself in situations where you are forced to interact with people who see the world very differently from you. Bring together a team of people with a broad range of expertise and experience to solve problems. Depending on the scope of the issue, consider bringing people together and asking them to discuss problems and solutions from their perspectives. Draw on other people to help address the big problems. Use them to expand your thinking. For example, a manufacturing company like Boeing regularly brings engineers and mechanics together in integrated product teams to figure out how to design new planes in a way that will minimize ongoing maintenance costs.

Build Real Time Reflection into Your Team

In your one-on-one meetings with your direct reports, take time to ask them what they are learning about the business and about themselves. Spend time during every team meeting having people share recent successes and new lessons. Model how important it is to you by beginning with your own lessons learned. Build milestones into projects when the team can consider what is working, what isn't working, and what needs to change in the future. At the end of projects, lead your team in an after-action review (see the box below) to model a learning culture and drive real time reflection at the team level.[3]

Create Organizational Systems That Require Reflection

Look for opportunities that will require different functions or business units to work together and share their insights. For example, assemble a task force of cross-functional teams to solve a pressing problem. It may be the launch of a new product or service that requires the collaboration of two established business divisions. The secret is to create the space where people are exposed to, and are expected to integrate, different perspectives. The regional VP in an insurance company, for example, used the yearly strategic planning

Tip:
After-Action Reviews

Set aside time at the end of a project to reflect on what worked, what didn't, and what should be done differently the next time. Even better, set aside time in the middle of the project or during key milestones to reflect on what is working well, what is broken, and how this information can be used in the next phase of the project. The focus should be on lessons learned, not on blame. Be careful what you name these sessions. For example, one organization commonly referred to them as "postmortems" and was then surprised that few, if any groups, took the time to do them! Who wants to talk about a project that's already dead and gone? The meetings should use past lessons to focus on the future. They should create energy. The leader's attitude will set the mood for these meetings. When this process is used in the military, a key condition is that "rank is left at the door" – *all* participants and all opinions are valued equally. Simple acts by the leader, like sharing some of his or her own shortcomings early in the meeting, can trigger more open dialogue. Bringing in an external facilitator to run the meetings can be helpful. Although leaders may be tempted not to attend, so that people feel more freedom to share their opinions, the meetings are significantly more powerful if the leader is there to model a learning-focused and open dialogue.

After-action reviews can be as short as 30 minutes for small projects or can last up to two or three days for large projects. They can vary in size from small teams to large teams to organization-wide teams made up of representatives from different departments.[4]

The goal of the meeting should be to address four broad questions:

- *What happened*: What did we expect to happen? What actually happened?
- *What worked well*: Why did it work so well? What should be continued in the future?
- *What didn't work and why*: What went wrong? Why didn't it go as planned?
- *What now?* How can we apply what we have learned to address the future challenges that we will face?

Ultimately, the success or failure of after-action reviews is measured by later actions. Is the organization better able to face future challenges?

process to accomplish this. The sales, service, and claims departments had been building their own strategic plans. Instead, he required that the plans in the coming year be developed for each customer segment, forcing the sales, service, and claims departments to work together to consider the total customer experience and costs.

All business processes offer opportunities to reflect. Business strategy meetings, quarterly business reviews, talent reviews, and year-end performance reviews are all opportunities to reflect on learning *if* reflection is intentionally incorporated and valued. If these meetings and reports are entirely about presentation and looking good, then little or no learning is likely to occur. If the discussion moves beyond just the raw numbers to an examination of why they are good or bad, and how that informs future directions, then learning is possible. So take a minute right now and reflect: How are these meetings run in your organization?

To Learn More

Argyris, C. (1991). Teaching smart people how to learn. *Harvard Business Review*, **69**(3), 99–109.

Baird, L., Holland, P., & Deacon, S. (1999). Learning from action: Imbedding more learning into the performance fast enough to make a difference. *Organizational Dynamics*, **27**(4), 19–32.

Ericsson, K. A., Prietula, M. J., & Cokely, E. T. (2007). The making of an expert. *Harvard Business Review*, **85**(7/8), 114–21.

Seibert, K. W. (1999). Reflection in action: Tools for cultivating on-the-job learning conditions. *Organizational Dynamics*, **27**(3), 54–65.

Chapter 9

When Leaders Derail

The Challenge

Nobody likes to think about career derailment, the term used to describe the involuntary cessation of a once advancing career. It feels like a train wreck for the individuals who derail and it's costly for organizations as well. The irony is that this wreckage sometimes represents one of the most significant development experiences for leaders.[1] Over the last three decades, I-O psychologists have learned a lot about the causes of derailment, how leaders can prevent derailment, and what they can do to get back on track when things go wrong. In this chapter, we'll discuss some of these key findings and how you can use this information to manage around your own weaknesses, help your direct reports, and build an organization that is derailment-resistant.

The Bottom Line

The Dynamics of Derailment

Derailment is most likely to strike during times of transition – a new boss, a new job, or a significant shift in the business environment.[2] Old strategies no longer work and past strengths can become weaknesses in the new conditions. For example, imagine the leader who moves from a staff finance position, where company-wide solutions are developed through collaboration and consensus, to a line leadership position in sales, where daily execution is what matters most. Suddenly, those collaboration skills and the inclination to look for shared group solutions become a liability. To survive, the leader is going to need to give up some of the very things that made him or her successful in the previous role, and is going to have to learn a whole new set of skills that have not been tested before.

But derailment doesn't only happen during a job change. The job can sometimes change underneath the leader. A new boss can be assigned with different priorities and values. Maybe the new boss no longer values what the leader brings. Maybe he or she is just a bad leader. Maybe the business environment changes around the leader. Imagine a leader whose core capabilities have centered on disciplined operational excellence going into an entrepreneurial environment requiring innovation and change. The old strategies won't work anymore, and unless the leader figures out how to develop new ones or leverages other people, he or she will be in trouble.

Why Leaders Derail: The 10 Deadly Sins

Research in I-O psychology suggests that the leading causes of derailment are poor performance, a failure to adapt to change, arrogance, unrecognized blind spots, the failure to build a strong team, the failure to build a network, poor working relationships, the inclination to avoid stretch assignments, unethical behavior, and just plain bad luck.[3] These 10 common causes of derailment are described in more detail in the box at the end of the chapter, which outlines some strategies to prevent them from becoming a problem for you.

Getting Over a Derailment Will Take Time

Derailing in your career is never easy, especially when it wasn't your fault. The anger and sense of loss take a long time to subside. Sometimes you never get over it. Finding your part in the story is hard work. It's easy to blame yourself for too much or to overlook the role that you did play. In these moments, it's important to get outside perspectives – people who you trust and who can give you honest, constructive feedback. It also means asking people who might not be your biggest fans to give you their feedback. You still get to decide what you want to own and what you want to reject, but you need to listen first. Many of the leaders we have talked to over the years have never fully gotten over derailments in their careers. Some find themselves still driven by past failures and injustices. The ones most at peace are the leaders who have done the hard work to think through past situations and to come to terms with what was unfair and unjust, the role they played, and how they want to live their lives in the future.

Stay Open to Learning

The secret to both the prevention of derailment and recovery from derailment is being open to learning. It requires asking your manager, peers, employees, and customers for candid feedback. It means asking yourself, "What truth am I blurring?" You may find some things that you just have to accept (e.g., you are good at execution but will always struggle with long-term planning). There will be other things that you can change but it will take a lot of work (e.g., you are hard-driving and abrasive or you naturally want to make everyone happy). And there may be other things that require you to put in the time to learn them (e.g., you need to learn to build and defend your budget). Sometimes learning means you finally come to terms with who you are, accept it, and decide what you are going to do with it from here.

Derailment Isn't Always Bad

Derailment can be an important time of self-reflection, for clarifying the things that really matter to you, for discovering your leadership principles and for identifying what you stand for. It may teach you some things about yourself that you didn't want to know. Derailment can help some leaders confront just how far from their values they have strayed. It's a chance to ask yourself the questions that will make you a better leader on the other side. When leaders plateau in their careers – and a narrowing pyramid means that almost all leaders eventually do – it can propel them to consider the role they play in other people's lives, and the contribution (and legacy) they want to leave in their current job. For some leaders, it's the only way to break the habit of defining their value based on their job and find their value elsewhere. The experience of being derailed often forces leaders to take stock of changing goals and priorities, and gives them a chance to be a different kind of person.

Taking Action

Figure Out What Will Get in the Way of Your Success

Consider your own strengths and weaknesses. Assess yourself against the leading causes of derailment in the "10 Deadly Sins" box. Use the reflection questions below to identify the factors that are most likely to trip you up.

Find your Achilles' heel. Think about the future career paths you would like to pursue. Get specific. What do you want to do in five years time? Identify the derailers that could get in the way. Identify the aspects about your personality, style, abilities, or proclivities that you know will become an issue. Set aside time to answer the following question, "Given that I eventually want to _____, what is it about me that will get in the way?"

Learn from the past. Consider a career setback that you have experienced in the past. Think back on the lessons that you took away from that experience. If a younger leader were going through a similar experience, what advice would you give him or her? Thinking back on the experience, how have you changed and become a better leader as a result? What were some red flags you missed? What, if anything, could you have done differently?

Discover your strengths (or weaknesses?). Write down your five greatest strengths as a leader. Because every strength can become a weakness,[4] identify how each of your strengths could get you into trouble. For example, finance and budgets may be particularly easy for you, but you get nervous and tentative when decisions need to be made in emerging markets where data isn't available. Maybe you pick things up quickly and get frustrated in meetings when people can't keep up with you. Walk through each of your strengths and identify situations where they could trip you up and become liabilities. Look especially for times when you will be tempted to rely too heavily on your strengths, ignoring other alternatives. This is likely to be especially problematic when you are under stress and are tempted to revert to the skills that always worked before! For each of these weaknesses, identify how you can get "good enough" or design a support system to compensate for the weakness.[5]

Reevaluate your priorities. Derailment is a great time to evaluate yourself and your values. If you are stagnating or plateauing in your career, it is a time to consider the things that are most important to you. Picture yourself in 20 years – older, humbler and wiser. Imagine this future-you comes back to give you some advice. What would the future-you say? If a younger leader were going through this experience, what advice would you give him or her? If advancing beyond your current position is not possible in the foreseeable future, what contributions can you make right where you are? What else is important in your life right now? What can you do, inside or outside of work, to stretch and challenge yourself?

Create Your Own "Early Warning System"

Find ways to guard against derailment. Make sure you sit down with your boss and clearly define "success" in your job. Don't leave it to chance. Define the explicit and implicit measures that will be used to assess your effectiveness. If your manager thinks you have done poorly or failed, ask your boss to clearly define what he or she will need to see to conclude that you are performing better in the future. Come to a joint agreement in writing if possible. Establish milestones along the way that will help you both determine if you are on track. Ask the people around you to give you feedback about how you are doing. Don't expect that they will seek you out when they see a problem. Ask them directly how you are doing and to provide feedback on any changes they have observed. Take advantage of any feedback systems that are already in place to assess your ongoing performance, including one-on-one meetings with your boss, leadership assessments like 360-degree feedback, and of course your business metrics.

Build a Derailment-Resistant Organization

If you are a senior organizational leader and/or the HR professional in charge of talent management in your organization, you also are responsible for creating "early warning" systems in the organizations that will allow people to detect problems and make corrections before it's too late. For example, some organizations use structured onboarding processes to help new leaders understand the challenges they will face in their new jobs. For established leaders, rigorous performance management systems or 360-degree feedback systems can give managers feedback about how they are being perceived by others. When senior leaders are ready to make particularly significant moves in their careers, many companies like Microsoft or IBM will interview peers, senior leaders, and their direct reports and use the information to provide in-depth feedback and coaching to the leaders. Several other processes that are discussed later in this book can play a critical role in helping leaders detect problems and self-correct before it's too late (e.g., mentoring, networking, performance management, development conversations, transition management).

Create a culture where "success" is defined more broadly than by just management promotions. For example, some organizations have created career paths for technical employees that provide advancement opportunities so management is reserved for people who want to be leaders. A derailment-resistant culture is one that recognizes the value of employees at every level in the company who are making great contributions. It is one that challenges people to find jobs they enjoy, where they can have an impact and serve others.

Finding ways to build a derailment-resistant culture and to prevent derailment *before* it happens is smart business! Carefully examine individual cases of derailment – what were the contributing individual and organizational factors? Figure out if it really was the person. Sometimes it's time to stop blaming people and to figure out what's broken in the system.

To Learn More

Kovach, B. E. (1989). Successful derailment: What fast-trackers can learn while they're off the track. *Organizational Dynamics*, **18(2)**, 33–47.

Lombardo, M. M., & Eichinger, R. W. (1989). *Preventing derailment: What to do before it's too late.* Greensboro, NC: Center for Creative Leadership.

McCall, M. W., & Lombardo, M. M. (1983). *Off the track: Why and how successful executives get derailed* (Tech. Rep. No. 21). Greensboro, NC: Center for Creative Leadership.

Van Velsor, E., & Leslie, J. B. (1995). Why executives derail: Perspectives across time and cultures. *Academy of Management Executive,* **9**(4), 62–72.

Good to Know:
The 10 Deadly Sins

The 10 deadly sins listed below are by no means inclusive of all of the possible causes of derailment, but they comprise some of the most common problems that can trip leaders up.[6] Every company is likely to have some unique ones they may want to add. The readings suggested in this chapter provide a deeper discussion of common causes of derailment and additional suggestions about preventing derailment in your career.

1. Poor performance. There are many causes of poor performance. Sometimes leaders don't take the time that's needed to clearly define with their boss the criteria for "success" in their current assignment. Sometimes they are simply a bad match for the job and don't have the required skills. Some leaders may be so focused on promotion to the next job that they fail to invest the energy and hard work that is needed to succeed in their current assignment. To prevent this from happening to you, focus on succeeding in your current job before you consider future career opportunities. Clearly establish the top priorities in your job and the metrics that will be used to assess your progress. Make sure that you and your immediate manager agree to this, and ensure these are the same criteria that are important to the other key decision makers in your organization. You may have to take the lead, proactively setting expectations about what is realistic. Solicit feedback from the people around you to assess how you are doing. If you are struggling, admit it to yourself

Continued

and find ways to work with your manager and others to turn things around.

2. Failure to adapt. Leaders are in the greatest danger of derailment during times of transition, including promotions to a new job, lateral moves to a new business group, or moves to a new company. But the leader doesn't have to move for transitions to be a factor. Leaders derail just as often when the environment changes around them and they don't adapt to the change (e.g., a new boss, a change in the market, or a reorganization). To increase your adaptability, assume that change is the rule rather than the exception; anticipate it and actively seek feedback from others about the company and about yourself so you can adapt. Include the exercises discussed in this book in your approach to your job, focusing special attention on the chapters in Parts II and III and chapter 19 on transitions.

3. Arrogance. Leaders are often called upon to take stands and drive changes that other people won't always like. Leadership isn't a popularity contest, but sometimes there is a very fine line between self-confidence and arrogance. Leaders who try to make everyone happy never will, but

leaders who ignore feedback can get blindsided. The media is filled with stories every year about arrogant leaders who drift into serious ethics problems. To guard against arrogance, test yourself at the most basic level: Do you consider yourself better and more valuable than the other people in your organization? Consider how you react and behave under pressure: Do people come to you with bad news? Are you short with people, defensive, abrasive, abusive? Don't try to answer these questions alone. You will need external perspectives. Identify people you trust at work and at home (people who will give you constructive feedback).

4. Blind spots. Blind spots can include weaknesses. They can also be an overreliance on strengths.[7] For example, the marketing leader who becomes a general manager will be tempted to see everything as a marketing issue, failing to recognize equally important and valid perspectives that other disciplines bring to the table. To avoid blind spots, surround yourself with a diverse group of people and proactively solicit their feedback. Take time to ask yourself and the people around you, "What am I missing?"

5. Failure to build a strong team. Leaders, by definition, succeed or fail through others, so failing to build a strong team can be a fatal error for a manager. Some leaders fail to build a strong team because, deep down, they don't really want to be a leader. They want the title, but aren't interested in the job. Other leaders fail because they staff their team with weak talent or build a team of people who are just like themselves. Some leaders build a team where team members compete instead of complementing each other. Other leaders fail to create the conditions that will make the team successful. Building a strong team is complicated, hard work, and a never-ending process. The endnotes contain suggested readings to help you build strong, robust teams.[8]

6. Failure to build a network.
Leaders can derail, especially in large organizations, if they fail to build a strong network across the company. Leaders with weak networks are more likely to derail because their careers become tied too closely to a single senior leader. They are limited in their ability to draw on people. Their names are less likely to come up when new opportunities emerge, and they have fewer people who know and can advocate for them. Because they also tend to be less aware of organizational politics, they are more likely to get

caught in turf battles and are less able to frame their work in ways that will be accepted. Chapter 13 provides strategies that leaders can use to strengthen their networks.

7. Poor working relationships.
Leaders get things done through other people. For some leaders, what starts out as a drive for results can become abrasive and arrogant. Over time, people quit coming to the leader with feedback or bad news. Eventually, the leader self-destructs or, worse, people actively sabotage the leader. Equally dangerous is the leader who tries to please everyone.[9] Leaders wouldn't be doing their jobs if they tried to make everyone happy, but there are some behaviors that are never wrong: respect for others, openness to feedback, integrity, humility, honesty, and wanting the best for others. Consider your working relations with the people around you. Are you honest? Are you approachable? Do you want the best for others? Do people trust you? Improving interpersonal skills is tough work. Find a mentor who has struggled with the issues and get his or her advice. Consider working with an executive coach. Recognize that change will take a long time, and then look for some small changes you can make today!

Continued

8. Avoiding stretch assignments. Stretch assignments are often double-edged swords. Leaders need to put themselves in stretch positions to discover, develop, and refine their leadership potential. Avoiding them will likely decrease future promotion opportunities. After all, when tough choices have to be made, companies will tend to choose leaders who have proven themselves in the fire. However, there are equally good reasons to avoid stretch positions. They are high risk and people fail in them. Early failures can follow leaders. There may also be personal reasons (e.g., family or health issues) for why you might not take on stretch assignments. So, ask yourself the following questions: In your career, what do you value most? What is the right choice for you at this stage in your life? What is the right stretch for you?

9. Unethical behavior. Unethical behavior can destroy leaders and the companies they lead. To prevent getting in trouble, consider the choices you make every day in the gray areas of your business. Make sure you know what your legal and ethical responsibilities are in your industry, in your role as a manager, and as an employee of the company. Then ask yourself, "Would I feel comfortable if this action was published on the front page of the paper tomorrow morning?" If it doesn't feel right, don't do it. Ask someone! And remember, that the truth almost always comes out – eventually.

10. Bad luck. Sometimes derailment is simply being in the wrong place at the wrong time – you get caught in company politics, you get a new boss who's truly awful, you are given an impossible assignment, the market changes, and your performance suffers. So it's time to pick up the pieces, figure out a way to let the anger go, and move on. When you can finally think straight, don't miss the chance to consider signals you may have missed or the role that you may have inadvertently played. Everybody knows leaders who blamed everyone but themselves. Don't let that leader be you. So, if bad luck strikes, ask the people to share their thoughts. Be willing to listen without being defensive. They may be wrong, but their perceptions can provide you some valuable insights. Finally, find people who have faced similar situations.

Part III

Drawing on Other People

Dynamic, continuous change has created organizations and careers that are boundaryless.[1] In this environment, people are increasingly responsible for their own career development. Relationships, both inside and outside of the organization, play a pivotal role in the ongoing development and effectiveness of leaders.[2] In all relationships, conversations are the common denominator. They can be done well or poorly. They can lead to development or stagnation. In chapter 10, we will discuss how you can increase the effectiveness of your developmental conversations. In chapters 11–13, we'll discuss the three relationships that are particularly important in the development and ongoing performance of leaders – role models, mentors, and networks.

Chapter 10

Development Conversations

The Challenge

The biggest challenge is that there never seems to be enough time in the day to have the kinds of development conversations that you want to have with the people on your team. But before you beat yourself up too much, let's look at some surprising research. Jennifer Kidd, at the University of London, asked 104 people to discuss significant career development conversations they had in their careers.[1] Unexpectedly, only 21 percent of the discussions were with a boss. Other managers, mentors, external advisors, HR professionals, friends, and work colleagues were responsible for the rest of the conversations. Equally surprising, only 7 percent took place within the formal appraisal or development process. It appears, then, that development conversations can happen almost anywhere with lots of different people. It's a matter of being available and turning a conversation into something that makes a difference. In this chapter, we discuss how *you* can get the most out of your development conversations – to develop yourself and to develop others.

The Bottom Line

Development Conversations Begin with Trust

The relationship matters. All of us are a lot more likely to listen when we believe the other person is committed to our success and has our best interests in mind. In trusting relationships, we are more open to tough feedback. Criticism is heard as advice about what is getting in the way of our long-term success. In the study mentioned above, the researchers asked people to discuss what made the conversations so effective. What was interesting is that people didn't talk about what the other person did; instead, they talked about the person's character. They said the conversations were valuable because the other person was honest, frank, nonjudgmental, and had their best interests at heart.[2] They valued someone who cared about them and was willing to push them hard. In other words, they trusted the other person.

High Expectations + Confidence + Autonomy = Self-Fulfilling Prophesy

Several lines of research suggest that managers can have a profound impact on the ongoing development of their direct reports.[3] The manager's expectations are especially important. Managers are in the best position to challenge employees to consider new possibilities, offer guidance, provide critical feedback, help them get back on track, and open future career opportunities. Research on the power of expectations and self-fulfilling prophesies began in the 1960s.[4] In these early studies, teachers were told that some students would show significant gains in IQ in the coming year. Unbeknownst to the teachers, the students had been randomly chosen. The results showed that these students did in fact make significant gains during the year. The next question was obvious – how did the expectations get translated into higher IQ? A closer look suggested that teachers tended to behave differently toward the students who were supposed to make significant gains that year. They called on the students more often, they didn't accept easy answers, they provided more feedback, and their feedback was more comprehensive. Research in I-O psychology suggests the same mechanisms play out in the workplace.[5] Managers tend to get the most out of people when they set high expectations, express confidence that the person can meet those goals, and give them autonomy to excel. Leaders can create an achievement culture by setting high expectations for all team members.[6]

Different People Will Have Different Needs at Different Times

Development conversations can take a variety of forms. They may focus on topics ranging from career planning to project management to ongoing problem solving to confronting employees about performance problems. Likewise, employee needs will vary widely. Some employees will just be starting their careers while others are nearing retirement. Some people may be settled into their positions while others are in the middle of a career transition. People also react very differently to feedback. Some will be defensive, others overconfident, while still others will lack any confidence at all. The good news is that there are some underlying principles that apply to everyone. Conversations that happen at four points during an employee's career are particularly important catalysts for development: job transitions, ongoing coaching, confronting performance problems, and career development conversations.

1 Job transitions. The transition into a new job is an especially powerful opportunity for development. People are significantly more likely to be open to learning and feedback during times of transition.[7] The role of the manager is critical. The best things to address during job transitions include: clearly defining the responsibilities and results expected in the new job and how "success" will be measured, identifying possible landmines to avoid, providing regular feedback, and creating an environment where it is safe for the transitioning employee to ask "stupid" questions. The manager is in the best position to give the new employee a chance to test new ideas and to provide early feedback if the leader starts to get into trouble. The manager also serves as a critical link to the rest of the organization, helping new employees to build their networks. The manager plays a critical role in either making the transition a powerful developmental experience or something that is merely survived. Because transition experiences are so powerful, they are discussed in greater detail in chapter 19.

2 Ongoing coaching. Coaching is the ongoing guidance, support, and advice that leaders provide to their direct reports. Coaching conversations are the daily opportunities that leaders have to push their people to be their best. The goal of coaching is to make people more effective. Coaching isn't about providing solutions, but about developing people who can meet future challenges on their own. Peter Heslin and Don VandeWalle at Southern Methodist University and Gary Latham at the University of Toronto identified three dimensions of coaching that are important: *guidance* – providing direction on performance expectations, helping to analyze performance, providing constructive feedback regarding areas for improvement; *facilitation* – acting as a sounding board to develop new ideas, facilitating creative thinking to help solve problems, encouraging exploration and new alternatives; and *inspiration* – expressing confidence, encouraging continuous development, and encouraging and supporting new challenges.[8] Coaching conversations are successful when they lead to better performance.

3 Confronting performance problems. Dealing with performance problems can be one of the hardest types of conversations to have, but they can also make a real difference in someone's career. The outcome is never certain. As every manager eventually learns, problems should be dealt with quickly and directly; there are ways to structure these conversations to increase the likelihood that they will lead to improved performance.[9] Beginning the conversation is often the hardest part. Managers should *define the problem behaviorally* (e.g., "In staff meetings, you are usually the first one to point out problems with other people's ideas, but seldom offer any support or other possible solutions"), *identify why the problem is important to the company's success* (e.g., "You are making a lot of people on the team angry and they are just shutting down during the meetings"), and *end with a partnering statement* (e.g., "You have some great insights that I'm worried aren't going to be heard. I want to figure out how we can make sure you are heard and considered a valued partner on the team"). From there, the conversation moves into an opportunity for you and the other person to explore root causes, perceptions, and possible solutions. This is the place in the conversation when your direct report should be doing most of talking since he or she is the one who needs to own the problem, understand the root causes, and own the solution. A good conversation ends with a clear plan of action and a scheduled follow-up meeting to assess if the problem has been resolved. Sometimes the issue will emerge again, and be the subject of multiple conversations. In the worse case, the person may need to be removed. Even this is better than what sometimes happens in companies: people never get the frank feedback they need to improve and fail by default. Honest confrontation is something that we all deserve.

4 *Career development conversations.* Career development conversations are focused on the person's long-term career goals. Annual career development conversations are a great place to start, but these conversations can happen anywhere, at any time. They may be triggered by a new opportunity – a coveted job opens up, a headhunter calls, or reorganization forces someone to redefine their position. Being available is what counts. Like every conversation, career coaching starts with the manager's commitment to and genuine interest in the other person. Conversations typically include a discussion of the person's long-term and short-term goals and opportunities, their strengths and areas for development, and next steps in their development. What career options are realistic? What isn't realistic? What other options are being overlooked? Good discussions are challenging and supportive. These are frank conversations about where the person's talents can best be used, areas for future development, weaknesses that are being overlooked, and strengths that the person doesn't even realize they have. The conversation should end with a discussion of next steps (e.g., development activities, future assignments, possible mentors, training programs) and a date on the calendar for a follow-up conversation.

Development Conversations Can Happen at Any Time

Development conversations are just as likely to happen during ongoing project discussions, over lunch, or in the hallway, as in formal one-on-one meetings. In a dynamic, global economy, most companies can't guarantee they will be in business 20 years down the road. Employees who have entered the workforce over the past two decades have recognized and even embraced this new reality: Every day is new, the organization will keep me as long as I add value, and I will stay with the company as long as they provide value and opportunities for me. This doesn't diminish the critical role that managers play in the employee's development, but it does mean that the conversations are likely to sound a little different. They are more likely to be discussions about the *match* between the employee's aspirations, skills, and potential, and the organization's strategic goals and workforce talent requirements. They are more likely to be driven by the employees and sound more like conversations between free agents and the owner of their current contract. Increasingly, the manager's role may be to: (1) help the person to find the place in the organization where their talents match what is needed, and (2) develop the skills that will position them for future opportunities.

It is important to know what makes feedback most effective. Not all feedback is equal. In fact, a review of feedback interventions found that one-third of the time, feedback actually led to *lower* performance![10] So what makes the difference? Research suggests that effective feedback includes the following characteristics: It is timely, structured, explorative, informative (to help the person understand why they performed well or poorly), contingent (dependent on the person's performance), focused on the performance not the person, and future-focused.[11] The box below defines each of these dimensions in more depth.

Taking Action

Develop Yourself

Model what you expect from others. Write your own development plan and schedule a conversation with your manager. Make daily development and ongoing feedback a regular part of your job. Consider your projects, roles, and responsibilities in the coming year. Consider how you can use them to develop yourself and position yourself for future career opportunities. Look over the characteristics of effective feedback outlined above. Think about the feedback that you receive in your job right now and in the projects that your team owns. What's missing and how can you improve the feedback that you are getting?

Assess the Quality of Your Development Conversations

Use the Development Conversations Checklist box to assess a recent conversation you had with one of your team members. Give a copy of the checklist to all of your direct reports and ask them to rate you as a way to hold yourself accountable. One final note: Don't ask the question unless you are ready to act on it. Your direct reports will be watching very closely to see how *you* handle feedback!

Tips:
What Makes Ongoing Feedback Effective?

The best ongoing feedback meets the following criteria:

Timely: The closer in time that feedback is given to the performance, the easier it is for people to tell what they are doing well or poorly, modify their behavior, and adapt. Complex situations are the one important exception to this rule. In these situations, frequent feedback can actually get in the way of performance improvement because it interferes with ongoing performance (it's distracting!) and tends to hide underlying patterns and trends. In complex jobs, challenge the person to look back over their performance for the last several weeks to understand what is really going on – root causes, underlying trends, and systemic changes that could account for the results. Then ask them to report back to you about what they found.

Structured: Feedback that isn't organized into some framework or scheme will feel random and meaningless. Feedback is most useful when it is presented in relationship to the big picture. For example, manufacturing costs are just numbers until they are compared against last year's costs, this year's budget projections, or competitor's costs. The feedback becomes most meaningful when it is considered in a larger framework like a lean manufacturing model where data about cycle time, rework rates, workflow analyses, and lifetime operating costs can provide new insights.

Exploratory: Feedback should be seen as an opportunity for the person and the manager to explore what's working, what isn't working, and why. In today's complex environments, the root causes are seldom obvious. The manager and his or her direct report are both likely to enter the conversation with strong opinions, but the best conversations are focused on exploring the problem together to find a solution together. Experimentation helps people learn.

Informative: The feedback should be informative, helping both parties to discover *why* things went well or poorly in the situation so they can figure out what future actions will lead to the best results in the future. Take the time to identify and solve the root causes behind problems instead of focusing on surface-level symptoms.

Continued

Contingent: Unconditional positive feedback doesn't work. People quickly discount it, and in the end, research suggests that it doesn't lead to improved performance. People learn from contrasts. Positive and negative examples allow people to see what works and what doesn't and to develop higher level heuristics that can guide their actions (e.g., what works under what conditions). Research suggests that feedback is most effective when people are not only told what they did wrong, but are provided guidance about what would be a more effective action in the future.

Focused on the performance not the person: We can learn a lot from the kindergarten teacher who reminds us that there aren't bad kids, just kids who do bad things. Feedback that is focused on the *person* (e.g., "You aren't a team player") creates defensiveness and consistently results in no change or decreases in performance![12] Person-centered feedback feels like an attack, threatens self-esteem, and in turn, actually shuts down thinking because the person become overwhelmed by emotion (e.g., anger, anxiety, fear). It creates lots of heat, but not a lot of light. In contrast, feedback that is specific and focused on *behaviors* ("You never refill the paper in the copy machine") is less likely to raise defensiveness. Behavioral feedback leads to discussions about root causes (the underlying causes of the behavior), perceptions (how the behavior is perceived by others), and into the exploration of possible solutions. Of course, there are no guarantees. The person may still react badly, but behavior-focused feedback will significantly increase the *probability* that the conversation will be constructive and result in positive change.

Future-focused: Feedback, especially negative feedback, creates a lot of energy and that can go in a lot of different directions including denial, blame, anger, or rationalization. A future-focused discussion channels and uses the energy to drive positive change. Consider your own reaction to the following two questions: "Thinking back over the last year, what is your biggest regret?" and "Thinking about the coming year, what is the one thing you want to do differently?" Both questions focus on change, but the latter is focused on the future and is a lot more likely to generate forward-looking action.

Career Development Conversations Checklist

Use the following checklist to plan for an upcoming development conversation and to assess your coaching skills afterwards.

Rating	Dimension	Why it is Important
Before the meeting		
	The employee and the manager prepared for the meeting.	Real improvement is possible when both the manager and employee have thought through the issues deeply.
	The manager and employee have regular conversations about the employee's development and this conversation is just part of that ongoing process.	Managers shouldn't rely on one conversation a year to discuss the employee's development. Real development is part of an ongoing process.
During the meeting		
	The organizational strategies and priorities were discussed along with future opportunities that might be a good match for the employee.	A discussion of organizational priorities can illuminate the most promising career paths in the organization for this employee.
	The conversation focused as much attention on the employee's strengths as it did on areas for future development.	The conversation should be balanced to motivate employees.
	The employee's weaknesses were discussed in the context of his or her future career aspirations and potential (i.e., things that will get in the way of the employee's success).	The conversation should be honest, dealing with tough issues but in the context of how to make the employee successful.

Continued

	The conversation focused the most attention on on-the-job development opportunities.	On-the-job development is where most development occurs.
	The employee, not the manager, drove the direction of the conversation.	Ultimately, employees own and are responsible for their development.
	The employee did most of the talking.	This is a good measure of who drove the conversation and who is most likely to leave with ownership of the outcomes.
After the meeting		
	Every development goal included a measure that could be used to assess if it has been reached by the end of the year.	The more specific the development goals, the more likely they are to be pursued and achieved.
	The conversation didn't go as expected.	This is a measure to see if both parties added value and if it was a true conversation without either person dominating.
	The employee *wanted* to modify his or her development plan based on the conversation.	This a good measure of how engaged the employee was in the conversation, and if he or she gained any new self-knowledge.
	The employee and manager would like to have more conversations like this.	This is the ultimate test of both the content and the tenor of the conversation.

Develop Others

Find ways to coach and develop people as a natural part of your job. Schedule one-on-one meetings with your direct reports throughout the year. Use these meetings as opportunities to provide support, find out how they are doing, solve problems, provide feedback, and discuss their career goals. Use the meetings to review employees' project plans, to expand their thinking, to set deadlines, and monitor results. Schedule time during the year to meet with your direct reports (at least one hour per person) to discuss their development plan and long-term career aspirations.

Build Development Into Your Organization

Leverage the talent management processes in your organization to build development conversations and feedback into your organization's DNA. Build a feedback-rich culture where people are *expected* to challenge and develop each other, and where people are told the truth and given a chance to improve. If you are a senior leader or HR professional, encourage managers to use opportunities like goal-setting meetings and performance appraisal meetings to discuss employee strengths, weaknesses, and areas for future development. Hold managers accountable for conducting development conversations with every employee. There will be grumbling. Some employees will complain that on the one hand you say they are responsible for their own development, and on the other hand you tell them that it's required. But the truth is that today, ongoing development is a business necessity just to stay competitive. Employees who aren't growing put themselves and the organization at risk.

To Learn More

Cannon, M. D., & Witherspoon, R. (2005). Actionable feedback: Unlocking the power of learning and performance improvement. *Academy of Management Executive*, **19**, 120–34.

DeNisi, A. S., & Kluger, A. N. (2000). Feedback effectiveness: Can 360-degree appraisals be improved? *Academy of Management Executive*, **14**, 129–39.

London, M. (1997). *Job feedback: Giving, seeking, and using feedback for performance improvement.* Mahwah, NJ: Lawrence Erlbaum.

Scott, S. (2004). *Fierce conversations: Achieving success at work and in life one conversation at a time.* New York: Penguin Group.

Chapter 11

Role Models

The Challenge

Who are your role models? Be intentional as you reflect on people who you regard as successful, impactful leaders – as well as considering what you are learning from observing individuals who are less effective. While clearly more pleasant to be around, positive role models (e.g., those demonstrating exceptional capabilities), influence you through the same mechanisms as negative role models. From both positive and negative role models you can learn new behaviors and increase (or decrease) the frequency of existing behaviors.

For better or worse everyone is a role model. What kind of role model leader are you? Reflect on your own key character traits and behaviors. Consider what people are learning from interacting with you and observing your actions and attitudes. Leveraging and translating wisdom from present-day role models into action requires conscious identification and continuous reflection. In this chapter, we'll discuss how you can learn from role models in real time and how you can be a role model for others.

The Bottom Line

Learning From Role Models is Powerful

People learn much of what they know by observing others – not through direct experience or formal education. Observational learning is well documented as an effective form of learning which is largely unconscious and strongly influenced by the relationship between the model and the learner. Observational learning is the opportunity to learn what works and doesn't work from a distance.[1] Unfortunately, people don't always capture the lessons that role models can teach. Research suggests that people learn the most from role models when they have identified what they want to learn (know what they are looking for), are exposed to both positive and negative models, take time to practice what they observe, and do this in an environment that supports the new behaviors.[2]

Identify Multiple Role Models

It is far more effective to leverage multiple role models as opposed to looking to one role model for everything.[3] While it may be easier to learn from people who are like you, or like you want to be, it is also useful to extract lessons from people who are very different from you. Look inside and outside of your organization. Pay particular attention to your current (and former) managers, as research suggests that you are most likely to identify these position holders as your role models. Consider family members and friends. Don't ignore historical figures who continue to teach us lessons (e.g., Gandhi, Eleanor Roosevelt, Martin Luther King, Mother Teresa, or Abraham Lincoln).

Become a Positive Role Model for Others

The best way to learn from role models is to be one yourself. After all, as a leader, you are a role model – for better or worse.[4] Former bosses often have a defining influence in the development of leaders. One-third of the time these are really bad bosses who teach unforget-table lesson about what *not* to do as a leader.[5] Your actions and behaviors can affect people more senior to you, peers, and especially the people who report to you. See Figure 11.1 to assess the kind of role model you are for others.

Taking Action

You Have to Pay Attention

Learning from role models doesn't happen by accident. Research suggests that when left to chance, people sometimes don't pay

Review the continuum below and decide if your actions more strongly correspond
to that of a Positive Role Model or a Negative Role Model.

Positive Role Model		Negative Role Model
Generally, I am proud of the way I handle stress and adversity.	○○●●●●●●	I tend to lose my temper and say things during tough times that I later regret.
When I disagree with decisions in my organization, I voice my concerns professionally.	○●●●●●●●	I sometimes feign support for things I don't agree with.
I take my role as a manager and team leader very seriously.	○○●●●●●●	I concentrate my efforts on product and/or client responsibilities; my management role is an add-on.
I treat people similarly no matter what their position or level in the organization. Despite the context and content of these relationships being different, I am the same person.	○○●●●●●●	I behave differently towards my direct reports, my peers, senior leaders. I take on different persona depending on who I interact with.
I keep challenging myself to learn new things.	○○●●●●●●	I don't challenge myself much intellectually or with new experiences any more.
I am optimistic and see the glass as half full.	○○●●●●●●	I have a cynical streak and tend to first notice the glass as half empty.
I acknowledge my mistakes and accept responsibility for them.	○○●●●●●●	There are usually good reasons for the mistakes I make (e.g., others' lack of effort or follow-through).

Figure 11.1 What kind of role model are you?

attention, they don't retain what they learn, and they don't always turn it into action.[6] So figure out what you want to learn, and find role models who live those lessons, translate them into something you will remember (e.g., link it to what you already know, write it down, tell someone what you plan to do), and practice it. One senior executive we know reflected that early in his career he worked for a miserable boss. He kept a black notebook in his car and captured all the things he vowed not to do should he ever attain a leadership position himself.

Consciously Identify Your Current Role Models

Adopt a holistic frame of reference. Look broad and deep within your networks to consciously consider who you are learning from and what you are learning. Reflect on your role models' behaviors and attitudes, especially during pivotal moments or experiences where leadership really matters. The box below lists the kind of situations where you should be scouting for role models. These triggers can serve to remind you to step back and observe others' behaviors and actions. But it's not just unusual or crisis situations that afford opportunities to learn from role models; everyday behaviors and attitudes can also be modeled.

Translate Learning into Action

Notice what your role models do and don't do. Ask them why they did what they did. The box below lists common categories of lessons that individuals are able to learn from role models. As indicated, the range of lessons to be learned is broad and diverse. To maximize your learning potential from role models, pay attention and make a point to stop and reflect on your specific take-aways from your role models. As mentioned in previous chapters, the ability to engage in self-reflection is important to furthering your own development. Be open to new ideas and new methods of getting things done. Listen, observe, and ask questions. Pick one or two behaviors that you will consciously incorporate into your own repertoire. Seek feedback from others. Consider connecting with colleagues who interact with the same role models as you do. Are you learning similar lessons? What actions and behaviors are salient to your colleagues that you might have missed?

Tips:
Identifying Your Role Models

The following questions can be used to identify the people who serve as role models in your organization. Review the list and add your own examples.

Crisis Situations

• Who steps up to take the lead during unplanned emergencies? Who was expected to step up?
• Who connects and engages with internal and external stakeholders? Who retreats away from people during a crisis?
• Who communicates messages of resilience and optimism? Who focuses only on negative attributes of situation?
• Who shares credit for the resolution? Who shares the blame?

New Clients

• Who initiates relationships with new clients?
• Who has solid, long-term relationships with clients?
• Who does the client phone? Who does the client want to interact with? Who do clients avoid?
• Who gains client trust quickly? Who do clients not trust?
• Who introduces new clients to others? Who hoards new clients?

Larger Role

• Who was promoted into a new or broader job recently?
• Who deserved to be promoted but was overlooked?
• Who took on a lateral assignment?
• Who stepped into a role outside of their comfort zone or area of recognized expertise?
• Who had a peer promoted over them?

Feedback

• Who is not afraid to have the difficult conversations? Who does this well? Who is brutal?
• Who provides positive feedback and support?
• Who asks for feedback?
• Who listens to feedback from direct reports, from peers?

Good to Know:
Lessons to Learn from Role Models

Basic Human Values	**Management Essentials**
Integrity	Delegation – you can't
Trustworthiness	manage everything alone
Humility	Employee advocacy
Fairness	Decision making
Ethical principles	Resilience – persevering
Acknowledging personal	through adversity
limits and blind spots	Developing other people
	Being tough when necessary
Interpersonal Skills	**Business Savvy**
Supportiveness	Thinking strategically
Effective communication	Innovative problem solving
Relationship building	Recognizing and seizing
Adaptability	opportunities
Openness to learning	Being results-oriented
Confidence, not arrogance	Being client-focused

Make Role Models Visible

Leverage opportunities to highlight positive role model leaders in your business or organization. It is a practical, inexpensive way of developing capabilities in others in the organization. Just be sure your role model leaders exhibit the desired skills, attitudes, and behaviors. For example, public acknowledgement of individuals who perform in a manner supportive of your desired culture can help focus the attention of others towards these individuals. Look for individuals who handle difficult situations well, or those who establish new client relationships, or those who coach and develop others. Invite role model leaders to be involved in key projects, or key initiatives in the organization such as diversity, philanthropy or leadership development. Be careful who you promote into senior management because it will signal what you value. Be conscious of any opportunity that arises to put someone in a spotlight, no matter how trivial it may seem at the time. Know others are watching and learning. And they are watching and learning from you too.

To Learn More

Badaracco, J. L. (1998). The discipline of building character. *Harvard Business Review*, **76(2)**, 114–24.

Gardner, H. E. (1995). *Leading minds: An anatomy of leadership*. New York: Basic Books.

Ibarra, H. (2004). *Working identity: Unconventional strategies for reinventing your career*. Cambridge, MA: Harvard Business School Press.

Weaver, G. R., Treviño, L. K., and Agle, B. (2005). "Somebody I look up to": Ethical role models in organizations. *Organizational Dynamics*, **34**, 313–30.

Chapter 12

Mentoring

The Challenge

In the last chapter we discussed role models and the importance they play in developing current and future leaders. Now we look at mentoring relationships which are typically one-on-one relationships, between leaders (senior–junior) or between colleagues (peer–peer).

Traditionally, mentoring has been based on an apprenticeship model whereby activities conducted by a person (the mentor) for another person (the mentee) were intended to help that other person to do the job more effectively. The mentor was someone with experience, someone who had "been there, done that" before. The challenge today is to not lose sight of mentoring's simple and practical foundations. The explosion of formal mentoring programs within organizations and professional associations, as well as advancement in technologies, may pull us away from the fundamentals of what it takes to effectively mentor and be mentored.

The Bottom Line

What Mentors Do

Who have been the people who have been important in your development? Research supports the positive impact that mentors can have on an individual's career progression.[1] Mentors don't guarantee new or expanded roles for the individuals they mentor, but they do open up new ways of thinking and new opportunities. Mentors provide guidance along the way by being supportive, asking probing questions, providing introductions to new people, and highlighting new opportunities. They serve as sounding boards and trusted advisors. Mentoring and coaching are different. While they both support individuals to attain their full potential, and the terms are often used interchangeably, they are distinct processes. Coaching typically refers to a time-bound relationship focused on specific performance-related issues. Mentoring, on the other hand, can stretch over an extended time and focuses on providing general advice and motivation regarding one's career and life. Mentors are typically experts or experienced professionals. Coaches are experts in questioning skills and in guiding individuals they work with to find answers for themselves.

Mentors offer career advice and guidance based on their experiences within a particular field or industry or job role. They provide constructive, thoughtful feedback. While effective managers do mentor, it is recommended that you seek mentors from outside of your immediate area of responsibility. Intercompany mentoring relationships can promote an understanding of the organization's culture. See the list of key questions below that mentors and mentees may explore.

The Power of a Developmental Network

Recent research suggests that people should move beyond looking for a single mentor and instead consider how they can build a developmental network of people in their lives.[2] The more diverse the better. A developmental network can provide a variety of role models who offer advice across multiple roles in the leader's life and a broad range of career opportunities. In effect, they can serve as the leader's personal "board of advisors."[3] They can include people at work, people in other organizations, and people in the leader's personal life. Some will be strong connections, some will be looser, but together they can offer more development than any single relationship might provide.

What it Takes to be a Mentor

Some of these relationships are likely to mirror a typical mentor–mentee relationship. The essential requirements for someone assum-

Key Questions to Explore	
Questions For Your Mentor	**Questions For Your Mentee**

• Describe the work experiences that made a significant difference on you as a leader.
  ◦ What did you learn?
  ◦ How did you learn these lessons?
	• Tell me about your current role.
	  ◦ What excites and energizes you?
	  ◦ What do you find draining?
	  ◦ What keeps you up at night?

• What do you wish you'd done earlier in your career but didn't?	• What have you done differently, more, or less of, since we last met?

• Who were/are your role models?
  ◦ What are you learning from them?
	• Who are your role models?
	  ◦ What are you learning from them?

• What questions are you asking yourself at this stage in your career?	• What are your interests outside of work?

• Describe a key work or personal challenge and ask:
  ◦ What factors would you focus on?
	• Tell me about your latest challenge.
	  ◦ What did you learn from this?
	  ◦ How did you learn those lessons?

• How do you manage multiple, often competing priorities?	• What are your core strengths?
• What advice do you wish someone had given you earlier in your career?	• What role do you see yourself in two to five years from now?

ing the role of a mentor are confidence in one's abilities and interest in someone else's growth. It is also important to be able to ask good questions and to be an effective listener, skills that are a natural extension of a real interest in another person's development. If questioning and listening are not your strong suit consider seeking feedback and guidance from your mentee; there are no rules suggesting that mentors give and mentees receive. In fact, some of the most effective mentoring relationships are interdependent, with mentors and mentees both reporting personal benefits as a result of their interaction.[4]

Be a Mentor and a Mentee

Research and practice suggest that the most effective mentors were themselves mentored at some point in their career.[5] Organizations should encourage people to play both roles. This is a powerful way of clarifying expectations for both mentors and mentees and furthering the culture of mentoring in organizations. Consider leveraging your high potential population to both serve as mentors and to reach out to be mentored by others. But don't wait for the company: Approach an individual whom you admire and respect. Share why you would like that person to be your mentor and what you hope to learn from having an opportunity to engage in a mentoring relationship with him or her.

Mentoring Takes Time

Mentors and mentees must both make an investment of time into establishing and maintaining a mentoring relationship. Lack of time is often cited as a reason for less than successful mentoring relationships. Using email and telephone calls can be an efficient way to stay in touch after the mentor–mentee relationship is established. Quality over quantity is an important consideration in mentoring – it is not realistic to mentor more than three individuals at a given time, especially for leaders who are in full-time demanding roles.

Taking Action

Build Your Own "Board of Advisors"

Identify a group who can serve as your personal board of advisors. They should come from a variety of roles in your life (e.g., work, community, family). Consider people you are close to as well as individuals you interact with infrequently. Push yourself to include at least two people whom you respect but who you are sure would never be interested. You don't have to ask them, but write them down. For each person, identify at least two pieces of advice you would like to gain from them. This is an important way for you to start articulating what you would like from others when opportunities and people present themselves. Remember that your goal is to build a developmental network of people. This is discussed further in the next chapter.

Find a Mentor

Some of the people in your network and on your board of advisors will be mentors. It's important to be intentional about how you build these relationships. Reasonable expectations for both parties involved in a mentoring relationship include: being in regular contact, keeping confidences, following through on commitments, providing candid feedback, and honoring the time investment of both parties. It is important to establish goals and objectives at the onset of a mentoring relationship, a responsibility primarily owned by the mentee. Do your homework by clarifying what you hope to gain from the relationship, considering your mentor's key strengths as you establish your own goals. What do you admire in the individual? For example, is it their client-management skills, technical expertise, leadership presence, people-management abilities, team-building skills, ability to manage commitments outside of work, experience base, or industry knowledge? Are you seeking general career advice or more specific guidance pertaining to your role? Will you ask your mentor to suggest and provide resources and/or introduce you to other people or will you use your mentor as a sounding board, someone to bounce ideas off? While the relationship will evolve over time it is useful to hone in on some specific goals during the first meeting. This is especially important for someone who has not been a mentor in the past and who may be feeling anxious about assuming the responsibility.

Understand the Mentoring Process

A typical mentoring process consists of a series of meetings over an agreed duration of time (e.g., once a month over 12 months). Generally the meetings are face-to-face. Even in the case of a virtual mentor–mentee relationship, some face-to-face time is important to establish the mutual level of trust that is required for most effective mentoring relationships. At the conclusion of each meeting, discuss what worked well and any opportunities for improvement. In addition, it is helpful to identify topics to be discussed in future meetings to enable preparation by both parties. Mentees should also consider ways that they can help their mentors (e.g., volunteering to work on a project with the mentor). Thank your mentor for their time and advice. See the box below for a list of general mentoring guidelines.

Create a Mentoring Culture in Your Organization

Because of the preponderance of positive outcomes associated with mentoring, many organizations have implemented formal mentoring schemes, but the research suggests that informal mentoring relationships tend to be the most effective.[6] This shouldn't be much of a surprise, since the chemistry between mentors and mentees is a critical aspect of a successful mentoring relationship.

You can't force a mentoring relationship to work. This leaves us with a bit of a problem: Mentoring is good but it has to emerge naturally. The good news is that there are ways that organizations can take this into account. To harvest the benefits that come with both formal and informal mentoring programs, create pools of mentors and mentees and facilitating opportunities for informal connections between individuals. Provide career profiles and personal data such as interests and hobbies of mentors and circulate them among the pool of mentees. Companies like Microsoft have created internal websites where employees can sign up as mentors or mentees. Individuals can sign up as a pair, or mentees can browse the profiles of possible mentors to find a good match. The site also provides a

Tips:
Mentoring Guidelines

- Mentoring relationships are voluntary.
- Either party has the right to withdraw from the mentoring process if, despite them genuinely trying to make it work, the relationship is not satisfactory.
- While often the mentor will have more experience of life or an aspect of work, the relationship is an interdependent one where both parties should give and receive value.
- The first meeting should focus on rapport and relationship building: background, current work focus, short-term and long-term aspirations, preferred mode of communication, and deciding on frequency of meetings.
- Meetings should be held in a quiet environment (or suitable environments for telephone meetings) where both parties can speak freely.
- Meetings should be long enough and paced so as to allow the two people to get to know and feel comfortable with each other.
- Information shared in mentoring meetings is confidential.
- Commitments made should be honored.
- If meetings are cancelled or delayed, adequate warning of nonavailability or delay should be given. Postponed meetings should be rebooked promptly.
- Either party has the right to ask for a review of how the mentoring is progressing or for agreements or plans made at an earlier stage to be reviewed.
- Notice to end the mentoring process should allow for at least one final meeting where closure (e.g., review/summary) can take place.
- Both parties accept that mentoring is for a limited period; the continuation of the relationship is entirely optional.

variety of tools and resources that participants can use to structure and support their meetings. To build a broader mentoring culture, provide visibility of individuals who are interested in mentoring others. Where mentoring is taking place, provide some general guidelines regarding the process of mentoring and briefings for mentors and mentees to ensure that expectations are managed. For some purposes however – onboarding would be a good example – formal mentoring is better, where assigning mentors is easy and has significant benefits to the person and the company alike. Most of all, remember that mentoring relationships don't just happen by matching two people up: They take work, and organizations need to be intentional and strategic in how they can systemically promote these powerful developmental opportunities.

To Learn More

The following books and articles provide more information about being a mentor and the mentoring process.

Ensure, E. A., & Murphy, S. E. (2005). *Power mentoring: How successful mentors and protégés get the most out of their relationships*. Hoboken, NJ: John Wiley & Sons.

Corporate Leadership Council (2005). *Mentoring from theory to action*. Washington, DC: Corporate Executive Board.

Ibarra, H. (2000). Making partner: A mentor's guide to the psychological journey. *Harvard Business Review*, **78(2)**, 146–55.

Chapter 13

Building Your Network

The Challenge

When you consider all of your priorities as a leader, both short-term and long-term, networking can too often fall to the bottom of the list. In fact, the term may conjure up images of playing politics, exploiting other people, or being a waste of precious time. Perhaps you view networking as a "nice to do" but not a "necessary to do" action. But if you look just beneath the surface of your priorities you'll realize that relationships with other people are key to accomplishing most, if not all, of your actions. So the first challenge is to shift your mindset from viewing networking in a negative light or as something to do in your spare time to thinking about its direct link to leadership effectiveness and getting things done. The next challenge is to understand who makes up your network and assess the strength of your network. For example, is it as broad and diverse as it needs to be? What can you do to improve and strengthen it over time?

The Bottom Line

Networking is Work

It is your network of relationships with other people that will provide you with support, insight, feedback, resources, and information that are critical to accomplishing your business goals and your continued career development. If you look around at the people who are most

successful in your organization, it's a good bet that the one charac-
teristic they have in common is their ability to develop and maintain
an interconnected web of trusting relationships. These relationships
provide them with access to information and an array of diverse skill
sets and ideas. More ideas and personal information create a source
of personal power and influence for those who leverage networks
effectively.

There Are Different Kinds of Social Networks

Herminia Ibarra, Chair of the Organizational Behavior program at
INSEAD, and her colleague Mark Hunter, provide helpful distinc-
tions between personal, operational, and strategic networks.[1] *Personal networks* are people you have something in common with and
who provide valuable referrals to useful information as well as supporting your personal development.[2] These individuals are the ones
who provide you with candid feedback and support. *Operational
networks* are people who help you get things done in your job and
represent the important stakeholders and groups at work. *Strategic
networks* are especially important in broader business leader roles.[3]
They include lateral and vertical relationships with other functional
and business unit managers outside of your immediate area of
responsibility. The people in this network should be internal *and*
external to your organization. The conversations with individuals in
this network tend to be oriented towards the future. Strategic networks are the ones most likely to be overlooked by aspiring leaders,
but they are precisely the relationships that are necessary to sell ideas,
compete for resources, lead, and accomplish your broad strategic
objectives. Personal, operational, and strategic networks do not need
to be mutually independent; in fact, people with the most effective
networks tend to leverage their personal and operational networks
for strategic information, ideas, and resources. You may also develop
friendships with people in your operational or strategic networks,
who will become important members of your personal network.

Networking is More About Will Than Skill

The good news is that everyone can build a powerful network. While
it does require time, networking is not reserved for those with

specialized skills or the "right" personality. In fact, you already have a network. Everyone does. Expanding and enhancing your network simply requires conscious thought and a few practical tips which are highlighted below.

Taking Action

Map and Evaluate Your Network

The first step in creating an effective network is to map your network (see the box below).[4] There are three questions to ask yourself as you evaluate your network: (1) Who are your key contacts? (2) How did you meet each contact? (Consider where you met them as well as who introduced you?) (3) Who have you introduced each of your key contacts to?

Mapping Your Network

Personal Network

Identify the people who are important in your personal development. These might include former bosses, professional colleagues, mentors, family members, or friends, among others.

Name of Contact	Where did you meet?	Who introduced you?	To whom did you introduce the contact?

Continued

Operational Network

Identify the professional contacts who are the most important in getting your work done. People in your operational network might include senior leaders, current and former bosses, peers, colleagues in other parts of the organization, clients, or suppliers, among others.

Name of Contact	Where did you meet?	Who introduced you?	To whom did you introduce the contact?

Strategic Network

Identify the people who help you think strategically about the future including colleagues in your organization or in other organizations, managers/customers/suppliers from other businesses, individuals from the community, or those associated with philanthropic concerns.

Name of Contact	Where did you meet?	Who introduced you?	To whom did you introduce the contact?

After you complete your network map step back and evaluate it. Identify gaps in your network map. Is there enough diversity in the people who form your network? Are there some people who you have not been in touch with for a long while? Don't forget to consider the areas where you have strengths. Perhaps you are an effective broker – someone who does a good job introducing your network contacts to others and connecting seemingly independent clusters of people together. Perhaps you have leveraged involvement in an organizationally sponsored community event to add to your personal or strategic network. Review the "Evaluating Your Network" box to assess the strength, breadth, and diversity of your network.

Build an Effective Network

Utilize your relationship-building skills to create mutually beneficial interactions with the people who are part of your current network. Expand and enhance your network one relationship at a time. Start with the groups and people that you naturally interact with at work. Focus special attention on the groups where you are the "bridge" from your group to another part of the organization. Consider other opportunities inside and outside of work. Leverage a personal interest or hobby by joining a group with similar interests, such as a running club, professional association, or a community project. Take the time to attend social functions at work such as retirement events, product launches, or internal conferences (especially those on topics outside of your own area of expertise). Practice your brokering skills by introducing the person you've been interacting with to someone else, which allows you to move on to meet new people. Find a reason to stay in touch with people and follow up. Complete the Effective Networking Assessment at the end of the chapter for other practical tips.

Leverage Your Network and Take Care of it

Networks that work for you and your business require active management. Seek out ways to interact with people in your network. Don't be afraid to make requests from those in your network and always be willing to provide assistance when others reach out to you.

Evaluating Your Network

Use the following questions to evaluate the strength, breadth, and diversity of your network.

1. I gain personal and professional value from my network.	Yes	No
2. I know what I have to offer the members of my network (e.g., skills, knowledge, information, influence).	Yes	No
3. I have been in contact with each of my network members within the last six months.	Yes	No
4. I leverage my personal network for feedback.	Yes	No
5. My operational network includes at least one member of each area or function I rely on to get things done.	Yes	No
6. At least two members of my strategic network are in more senior roles than I am.	Yes	No
7. Other people introduced me to my contacts at least 60% of the time (indicating that I am effectively leveraging other people to help expand my network).	Yes	No
9. I've introduced my network members to at least one other person.	Yes	No
10. I have strong ties to the people who have brokered many of my key contacts.	Yes	No
11. I am pleased with the diversity of my network. Individuals in my network consist of people from:		
• Multiple age ranges (e.g., same age as me, older, and younger)	Yes	No
• Varied cultural and ethnic backgrounds	Yes	No
• Multiple disciplines	Yes	No
• A variety of industries	Yes	No
• Various stages in their career journeys (e.g., early stage, senior leaders, retired).	Yes	No

Scoring: If you answered "yes" to at least 10 of the questions, you are well on your way to building a strong network! If not, choose one of the items on the list that you didn't check and begin to expand your network today.

Remember to acknowledge and appreciate contributions from people in your network. Look for opportunities to give and take information to and from your network. Don't wait for a crisis situation or times when you are in desperate need of information to leverage your network; rather make it part of your routine. In fact, tending to your network should regularly show up on your list of short-term and long-term priorities. Start today: Make a simple request of someone in your network or connect two people who don't know each other.

Help Your Team Build Their Networks

Be a good role model to others by helping your team members build their own networks. Connect them with the right people in the organization, set up cross-functional teams to tackle problems and process improvements, and model good networking so the people around you can see the value.

To Learn More

The following articles and books offer practical suggestions for building and maintaining a strong network:

Cross, R., Liedtka, J., & Weiss, L. (2005). A practical guide to social networks. *Harvard Business Review*, **83**(3), 124–32.

Cross, R., & Parker, A. (2004). *The hidden power of social networks.* Cambridge, MA: Harvard Business School Press.

Gladwell, M. (2000). *The tipping point: How little things can make a big difference.* Boston: Little, Brown and Co.

Ibarra, H. & Hunter, M. (2007). How leaders create and use networks. *Harvard Business Review*, **85**(1), 40–7.

Uzzi, B. & Dunlap, S. (2005). How to build your network. *Harvard Business Review*, **83**(12), 53–60.

Tips:
Effective Networking Assessment

Use the following scale to identify how frequently you engage in each of the networking activities described below. A scoring key is provided at the end.

1 = Never   2 = Occasionally   3 = Frequently   4 = Always

_____ 1. I reach out and provide information to people in my network.

_____ 2. I remember to acknowledge and say thank you for the information, resources, and ideas that my network provides me.

_____ 3. I organize my thoughts before making calls to people in my network.

_____ 4. I introduce myself in a way that is clear, concise, and engaging.

_____ 5. I am an active member of at least one professional and/or community association.

_____ 6. I accept invitations to participate in multidisciplinary events such as conferences, seminars, workshops, and speaker series.

_____ 7. I reintroduce myself to people rather than wait for them to remember me.

_____ 8. I remember people's names and facts about them.

_____ 9. I proactively introduce members of my network to each other.

_____ 10. I make notes on business cards I receive to act as memory joggers.

_____ 11. I volunteer to sit on task forces or committees to get to know senior managers and peers from other functional areas.

_____ 12. I generally return phone calls and email within 24 hours.

_____ 13. I ask for assistance/guidance from people in my network.

_____ 14. I regularly attend company social events.

_____ 15. I find opportunities to ask others: "Who do you know who . . . ?"

_____ 16. I regularly re-evaluate my network.

_____ 17. I actively seek ways to expand the diversity of my network.

_____ 18. I operate with integrity and professionalism in my interactions.
_____ 19. I consciously think about expanding and strengthening my network as part of my normal routine (e.g., I don't wait for special "networking events").
_____ 20. I help others develop their networks.

_____ **Total**

Scoring Key

Your total score provides an indication of your use of effective networking practices.

71–80   You are a networking role model for others. Continue to leverage your network professionally and personally.
51–70   You engage in many effective networking practices. Identify your strengths and build on them.
31–50   Some of your actions represent that of an effective networker. Look to increase practices that you use only occasionally. Consider incorporating practices that you "never" employ.
20–30   You may not be investing enough time and energy into building your networking. Identify practices that you don't currently use and commit to applying them.

Part IV

Building Experiences into Talent Management

S trategic HR systems are most effective when they are aligned verti-
cally with the corporate strategy and horizontally with each other.
Leadership development, especially experience-based development,
is exponentially more effective when organizational talent management systems support it. In Part IV, we discuss five talent management processes that are particularly important as you build a strong
leadership pipeline and a broad base of talent all through the organization. As a senior business leader or HR professional, these are
your best tools to drive systemic change in the organization, to lead
from wherever you are in the organization.

Chapter 14

Individual Development Plans

The Challenge

In too many organizations, development plans have become little more than paperwork required by the HR department. That is unfortunate. If most development does occur on the job, then development plans are one of the best tools to help people capture this learning. We propose that the single best strategy you have at your disposal to drive on-the-job development into the DNA of your organization is to encourage *all* employees to create an individual development plan (IDP). We also propose that you can build a development planning process that employees *want* to do!

The Bottom Line

Just Setting Goals Can Make a Difference

The simple act of writing goals down can trigger development. For example, the power of goals to direct behavior can be seen in a now classic management study at AT&T that followed the progression of leaders over a 20-year period. The single greatest predictor of who would eventually become an executive was their early ambition to be an executive.[1] (Having this goal was a better predictor than cognitive ability, interpersonal skills, personality, or even their early management skills.) Studies in I-O psychology with hundreds of participants have consistently confirmed that difficult, yet attainable, goals are one of the strongest predictors of later behavior and performance.[2] Articulating the goal directs attention toward opportunities that otherwise might be missed and creates a tension between what is and what could be, motivating people to seek their future goals.

Keep it Simple

Development plans don't have to be complicated. Your goal should be to create a simple process that people *want* to do. In its simplest form, ask people to write out their answers in three broad areas: (1) their long-term and short-term career goals, (2) their strengths and areas for development, and (3) the developmental activities that they

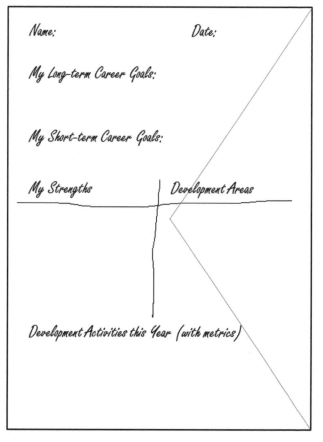

Figure 14.1 Keep it simple!

will pursue in the coming year (on the job, with other people, and in formal training). The forms can and often do get a lot more complicated – so much so they can begin to feel like a tax return. If the choice is between a sophisticated form that nobody uses and notes on the back of an envelope, go for the envelope! The real value is in provoking employees to take time at least once a year to ask themselves, "Where am I and where do I want to go? What are my strengths and what do I need to improve or develop? What specific actions do I need to take in the coming year to begin moving in the right direction?"

Make it So Compelling That People Want To Do It

To test just how compelling your development planning process is, ask yourself two questions: (1) "Did I create a development plan for myself last year?" and (2) "Did my employees want to create development plans for themselves last year?" If you don't feel that the process was valuable enough for you to participate, and if employees don't feel that they own it, something is wrong. The development planning process should be structured and communicated in such a way that employees see its inherent value.

The truth is that employees today are foolish if they leave their development in the hands of their employers. Organizations today can't guarantee long-term employment. Markets are too dynamic. Most companies can't guarantee *they* will be in business 10 years from now. The development planning process should reflect this reality. Make sure all communications about development planning are written from the perspective of the employees; that is, create a process that will help them manage their career. The items in the Development Plan Checklist box below were written with this in mind. Take, for example, the item, "I am developing skills that will be in demand three to five years from now." It would be crazy for people *not* to do this. It's in their best interest.

In this new reality, organizations and the employee's manager still have important roles to play. The *organization* needs to provide the processes, resources, and a culture where employees can grow. *Managers* need to provide coaching and feedback to employees. But these two roles should never dilute the message that *employees* are ultimately responsible for their own development.

Individual Development Plan (IDP) Checklist

This assessment can help you measure the quality of your development plan. Put an *X* next to the statements that are true. A scoring key is provided at the end.

Align Your Development with the Business Strategy

	My development plan will help develop my skills and achieve my business goals at the same time.
	I am developing skills that will be in demand three to five years from now.
	At least 70 percent of my development activities are linked to on-the-job development.
	This development plan will push me to the edge of my comfort zone in the areas I have targeted for development.

Discover Your Potential

	I get excited when I look at my development plan for the coming year.
	My plan focuses as much energy on developing my strengths as it does on improving my weaknesses.
	I feel that I am making a difference in my work.

Hold Yourself Accountable

	For each development goal, I have included a metric to assess whether the goal has been reached.
	I have recruited at least two people to hold me accountable to my goals.
	I have identified milestones throughout the year to ensure that I am on track.

Your Score	What it Means
0 to 4	You are in danger of finishing the year less employable than when you began. Look for a block of time (at least two hours) over the next two weeks when you can seriously focus on your development and discuss it with your manager. Your future is worth it!
5 to 7	You have a good development plan, but it needs some work. Look at the items you did not check and modify your plan accordingly.
8 to 10	You have created a strong development plan that will challenge you to develop your skills in important areas, positioning you to take advantage of future opportunities in your career.

Highlight On-the-Job Development

Unfortunately most employee development plans are simply a list of training programs that the person plans to attend, even though we know that the bulk of development is on the job. To succeed, today's leaders and employees need to focus their energy on self-directed, continuous development.[3] To help drive experience-based development plans, consider creating a list of on-the-job development activities that employees can build into their jobs based on the experiences (see chapter 1), relationships (see chapters 3, 10–13), and stretch assignments (see chapter 6) discussed in this book. On the development form, you might create a box next to each development goal (see "Developmental Assignments" box below) where employees are asked to indicate the type of development activity, including some guidelines on the percentage of activities that should fall into each based on the research[4] – on-the-job development (70%), other people (20%), training programs (5%), outside development experiences (5%). The best development plans should be linked to a person's performance goals for the year. In the best situations, it's not development versus performance, it's both! People take on challenges that are critical to the company, and use the experiences to grow their leadership potential.

	Developmental Assignments	
Identify three to five developmental goals for this year. List the activities on the right, write in a date by which you expect to have met the target, and then mark the kind of development activity it represents. Your goal is to have a development plan that is consistent with research about where development occurs.		
Developmental Activities	**Target Completion Date**	**Type of Activity**
		❐ On-the-job dev. (70%) ❐ Other people (20%) ❐ Training (5%) ❐ Outside work (5%)
		❐ On-the-job dev. (70%) ❐ Other people (20%) ❐ Training (5%) ❐ Outside work (5%)
		❐ On-the-job dev. (70%) ❐ Other people (20%) ❐ Training (5%) ❐ Outside work (5%)

Separate the Performance and Development Processes

"Now, wait a minute!" you think. "Didn't you just say the two should overlap?!" It is true, the best development assignments should be the ones that allow leaders to execute the business strategy and stretch themselves at exactly the same time. However, we recommend that you have *separate conversations* about performance and development goals. When the two conversations are combined, managers and employees, quite predictably, spend most of the time talking about the employees' performance goals for the coming year. If they do talk about development, the conversation is usually rushed and not very deep. A second problem can also occur. The end of the form, often labeled "employee development," becomes the repository where employees dump all the extra things they want to do in their job. Separate meetings give both parties a better chance to give both topics equal attention. For example, many organizations start the year with performance goal setting, discuss employee development six months later, and end the year with performance reviews.

The Conversation Matters!

Development plans are important, but they're just another piece of paper until they are put into action. The conversation is an opportunity for the employee and manager to identify future developmental assignments, to discuss possible mentors, and to negotiate resources that may be needed (e.g., travel costs to interact with stakeholders). The manager can provide an outside perspective and candid feedback about the employee's strengths and weaknesses. The conversation becomes a way for employees to establish accountability for action. However, the conversation is important well beyond these functional reasons. It is an opportunity for managers to show their confidence and belief in employees. Remember, beyond the employees themselves, managers are the ones who will have the next greatest impact on the development and performance of their employees.[5]

Taking Action

Challenge Yourself

Do a quick self-assessment to see if you are living up to the same goals you are expecting of your direct reports. Did you create a development plan for yourself this year? Did you meet with your boss to discuss it? If you haven't taken your development as seriously as you should, pull your development plan out of your file cabinet, blow off the dust, and schedule some time to think about what you need to do in the coming year to develop yourself. If this feels like too much work, go to a coffee shop, sit down, and jot down some notes on a piece of paper. Then assess what you have written against the Development Plan Checklist. How did you do?

Challenge Your Team

If your organization already has an employee development process in place, schedule time on your calendar to meet with each of your direct reports to discuss their plans. If performance goal setting and development goal setting happen at the same time in your organization, schedule two separate conversations to discuss the topics. Spending one extra hour per employee per year to discuss their career aspirations and development goals is a small price to pay when compared to the potential pay-offs. After all, your direct reports may consider this one of the most important conversations they have with you during the year.

Create High Quality Development Plans

Hand out the Development Plan Checklist and encourage your direct reports to assess their development plans before they meet with you. Make it part of the corporate development form or website. Make on-the-job activities a central part of every employee's development plan. Look for business challenges, assignments, roles, and responsibilities that will stretch your direct reports. Connect them with mentors and advisors in the organization.

Evaluate the Quality of Your Development Plans

Make sure that every employee development goal is specific and includes a metric to assess whether it has been obtained. Make sure that employees focus on both their strengths and their weaknesses. Have HR audit a random sample of development plans to assess their quality. Some of the things to look for might include: the percentage of developmental activities that are on the job, people-based (e.g., mentors), formal training, or activities outside of work. Remember your goal is to reflect the reality we know from research (i.e., 70% of development will occur on the job, 20% from other people). The audit could also assess: the percentage of activities that include a metric and due date; the percentage of activities focused on strengths versus weaknesses; and the percentage of plans that identify the experiences, competencies, and relationships that you identified in the beginning chapters of this book. Discuss the results with the leadership team and the employees in your organization. Use it as an opportunity to help people improve the quality of their plans and accelerate their development in the coming year.

What Do I Do When Employees Just Don't Care?

For some people a job is, well, just a job. Some employees are good at what they do, enjoy it, and, for a variety of reasons, aren't really all that interested in writing development goals for the coming year. For example, some may be close to retirement: They want to contribute in their current job, but why should they develop? They're retiring! For other people, their job may just be a way to support their family or a means to pursue other interests outside of work. Some workers are happy right where they are. Imagine the 20-year veteran schoolteacher who loves his job, or the first-level supervisor who likes what she's doing and is good at it. There are some ways to make the process more interesting and useful for even these people. For experienced workers, encourage them to set a goal to mentor others. For people who are coasting when they probably shouldn't be, challenge them to consider how things are changing in the industry and what they will need to do to ensure they are still employable in the years to come. For workers who feel plateaued or stagnated in their careers, look for special assignments that can add variety to their jobs. Encourage them to consider a lateral move into a new area. Where appropriate, encourage them to include developmental goals outside of work that will prepare them for the next stage of their lives. In the end, you might find yourself back where you began: In today's business environment, employees ultimately own their own development and have to make their own choices.

To Learn More

Chappelow, C., & Leslie, J. B. (2002). *Keeping your career on track: Twenty success strategies.* Greensboro, NC: Center for Creative Leadership.

McCauley, C. D., & Martineau, J. W. (1998). *Reaching your developmental goals.* Greensboro, NC: Center for Creative Leadership.

Stringer, R. A., & Cheloha, R. S. (2003). The power of a development plan. *Human Resource Planning,* **26(4)**, 10–17.

Yost, P. R., & Plunkett, M. M. (2002). Turn your business strategy into leadership development. *Training and Development,* **56(3)**, 48–51.

Chapter 15

Performance Management

The Challenge

The performance management process plays a critical role in leadership development, whether companies recognize it or not. Unfortunately, in the midst of day-to-day pressures, leaders are often so focused on the results that they miss the learning. But performance management systems can be structured so they drive high performance *and* develop leaders. The challenge is to perform – and learn. In this chapter, we discuss the elements you can build into your performance management system to achieve these dual goals.

The Bottom Line

Create a Performance Management Process That Works

The primary purposes of performance management systems will always be: to drive business strategy; to engage, motivate, and reward employees; to hold people accountable; and to ensure that everyone is treated fairly.[1] Too many organizations don't even have these basic elements in place. However, four other elements are needed for a performance management system that also builds strong leaders: well-written performance goals, ongoing feedback and coaching, rigorous evaluation, and a reward system that reinforces *both* performance and development.

Strong performance goals. Chapter 6 discusses the characteristics of a strong goal (i.e., specific, difficult yet attainable, with feedback). The box below provides an example of a well-written performance goal.[2]

Example: Effective Performance Goals		
Definitions		
Goals: Create goals that are specific and challenging (difficult yet attainable).	**Performance Plan**: Outline the key steps that will be needed to accomplish the goals.	**Metrics**: Identify the metrics and deliverables that are expected (including metrics to assess whether the project is on track).
Example		
Build and launch the new online site by 30 June with 10,000 average transactions and $100K revenue per month by the end of the fiscal year.	Key Steps • Create and test development site • Launch production site • Launch advertising campaign	Deliverables • Development site fully functional (by 30 March) • Production site fully functional (by 30 June) • Launch advertising campaign (by 31 July)
	• Assess site effectiveness and develop plans for V2.0	Metrics • Website development costs at or below budget • Customer transactions per month (Goal: 10,000 by the end of the year) • Online revenue (Goal: $100K/month by end of year)

Most companies talk about how important it is for all employees to set goals for the year, but it is amazing how often this doesn't happen. Taking care of day-to-day crises can be so overwhelming that leaders never quite get around to establishing yearly goals. Beyond the rather frightening legal risks (e.g., making reward decisions at the end of the year without documentation to justify them), development opportunities are also lost. Yearly performance goals challenge leaders to think through both the results they want to achieve in the coming year and the ways they can use the assignments to develop their leadership capabilities.

Ongoing feedback and coaching. The performance management process should include regular feedback and coaching throughout the year. For example, ongoing one-on-one meetings between managers and employees can be used to discuss project status, emerging challenges, and support needed to reach goals. When used for development, these meetings move beyond the work to also discuss the overall company strategy and why actions should or should not be taken. Leaders are challenged to move beyond the current problem and think about larger systemic issues, and how they are (or are not) developing their leadership skills in the midst of those challenges. Managers can also create the conditions for team members to challenge and coach each other. This can be modeled in staff meetings and become a natural part of the culture. Think back to your last staff meeting. Did you only discuss deliverables or did you make time to discuss what you are learning as a team?

Rigorous evaluation. Effective performance management systems hold people accountable for the results and how they got those results. As noted in earlier chapters, leaders develop the most in situations that stretch and push them to the edge of their comfort zones. Rigorous evaluation creates the pressure and visibility to support strong developmental experiences. Weak performance systems don't hold leaders accountable and don't provide the rich feedback about what leaders did well and where they failed to meet expectations.

Reward systems. Reward systems send strong messages about what is really valued in the organization. Steven Kerr points out in his article "On the folly of rewarding A, while hoping for B" that often what is publicly proclaimed as important is not what actually gets rewarded.[3] For example, organizations might say that people are their most important asset, but they promote leaders who get results at any cost. Reward systems should measure and reward how well leaders are developing the people around them.

Some of the indicators to watch include: the ability of managers to attract strong talent to their groups; on-time completion rates of performance goals, development plans, and performance evaluations; the number of employees from the manager's group who are promoted; and employee attrition rates. Some organizations collect employee feedback informally (see sample e-mail below) or through

---

Example:
Email Evaluation

To: [All direct reports, 1–2 senior managers, 2–3 peers, internal/ external customers of the group]
Subject: Feedback on Paul Yost

Dear _____,

I would value your feedback as one of Paul Yost's direct reports, peers, or customers, as I evaluate Paul's performance over the last year and think about his future development. Please take a few minutes to answer the following questions and reply directly to me. Your comments will be combined with other feedback to identify common themes. All comments will be kept confidential.

Thank you in advance for your help,

Mary Mannion Plunkett

Feedback Questions:

- In what capacity have you worked with Paul in the previous year?
- What, in your experience, are his greatest strengths?
- What, in your experience, are some areas for future development?

a more formal process like 360-degree feedback systems. Formal ratings can be extremely challenging when used for evaluation given how threatening it is for employees to rate the boss who, in turn, will rate their performance at the end of the year. However, this can be a valuable source of feedback about the leader's ability to manage and develop others *if* it is done well in a supportive organizational culture. If used, several precautions will need to be taken to protect employees (i.e., ensure it is anonymous, know that ratings will be inflated, protect employees against retribution from managers with low scores, determine what you will do if only a few employees respond, etc.).[4]

Make the Performance Management System Fair

Unfair treatment of employees will poison all other talent management processes. People generally consider three dimensions when they are determining whether an organization treated them fairly.[5] *Distributive justice* is the perception that outcomes have been distributed equitably (e.g., the ratio of one's contribution to one's output in comparison to other people). *Procedural justice* is the belief that the process is fair (e.g., it is applied consistently across people and across time, free from bias, based on accurate information, conforms to accepted ethical standards, and includes an appeals process for inaccurate decisions). *Interactional justice* is the perception that people in the process have been treated with respect, dignity, and politeness, and the perception that people were given accurate and honest information about why outcomes were distributed in a certain way. Guidelines on how to build fair and legally defensible performance can be found elsewhere.[6] However, here are some of the basic principles to keep in mind:

- Clearly explain the purpose of the performance management system, how the process works, and key deadlines, using a variety of communication channels.
- Hold managers accountable for completing each step along the way (e.g., setting performance goals, midyear performance checks, end-of-year performance evaluations).
- Document clear performance goals and measurable outcomes.
- Ensure that all employees are treated fairly and consistently.

- Use multiple raters wherever possible to obtain a more accurate performance assessment (e.g., require that all ratings are reviewed by the manager's boss and use "calibration meetings" to bring managers together to assess pools of employees who hold similar jobs).
- Give poorly performing employees timely feedback so they have the opportunity to correct their performance.
- Document, document, document – both good and bad performance throughout the year.
- Ensure the organization has a formal appeals process.
- Evaluate the process yearly to ensure that all employee groups are treated fairly (e.g., there isn't any systematic bias against specific groups).

Don't Let Performance Push Development Out of the Way

Some organizations have combined their performance management and development discussions into one process for greater efficiency. As noted in the previous chapter, performance issues will tend to dominate these conversations if you don't create a separate space for development. To ensure that development is addressed, consider scheduling separate meetings to discuss performance and development goals. Successful organizations are committed to great performance today, *and* to doing it in a way that positions the company to thrive tomorrow.

Taking Action

Develop Yourself

Use the performance management process to develop yourself. Look for stretch assignments that are critical to your business and will develop your leadership potential at the same time. Approach your ongoing assignments in ways that will force you to develop new leadership capabilities. For example, find "excuses" to work more closely with other people and other departments that will stretch you to think and lead in new ways. Ask people for feedback about your performance and about your leadership. Include a performance goal on how well you are managing and developing your team.

Develop Your Employees

At the beginning of the year, meet with all of your direct reports to set performance and development goals. Make sure they are stretching themselves in the year ahead. Think about the upcoming projects on the horizon. Consider who can best do the work *and* who can best develop from doing it. Assign the work based on both criteria. Meet regularly with your direct reports throughout the year to discuss project status and provide ongoing coaching. For every goal, encourage your direct reports to include metrics that will allow them to monitor and assess their ongoing progress. Require the leaders who report to you to include a goal on how well they are managing and developing their people.

Watch Your Biases

Psychology tells us that people create "schemas" that help us to simplify and categorize the world around us. For example, while no two houses are exactly the same, this doesn't stop us from understanding the general concept of "house." For the most part, schemas are helpful and adaptive, but they can become problematic when applied to people. We call them stereotypes. As a manager, you need to be aware that these biases are built in and take over if you don't guard against them. Some of the especially powerful ones include: the *halo error* – a tendency to form an overall impression of an employee that colors everything else; the *"similar to me" bias* – a tendency to rate people higher who are similar to you; the *primacy* and *recency effects* – biases to weigh early performance and end-of-the year performance more heavily; the *contrast error* – a tendency to compare people to each other; and *stereotyping* – letting someone's group membership affect your ratings.[7] As you think about your direct reports, be careful that your initial judgments don't color all your later judgments. Ask yourself at the end of the year how your judgments of each of your direct reports have changed. If the answer is "not at all" go back and look again. What are you missing? Document their performance throughout the year and refer back to your notes at the end of the year. Make sure you are rating each performance goal separately. Know the laws in your country and the rules in your organization. Ignorance won't keep you or your company out of court.

Walk the Talk

Make sure you set your own goals for the year. It's startling how many mid-level and senior-level leaders require goals for people that work for them and yet don't have any of their own. In team meetings emphasize the importance of execution against goals, and discuss your goals and what you intend to learn along the way. In our experience, one of the most powerful symbolic acts that senior managers have made is to publicly admit they performed short of expectations during the year and will be rewarded accordingly, just like any other employee. Model a fierce commitment to execution, a willingness to tell the truth, and the ability to learn from your mistakes. Challenge every team member to do the same.

To Learn More

Aguinis, H. (2008). *Performance management*, 2nd edn. Upper Saddle River, NJ: Pearson Prentice Hall.

Kerr, S. (1995). On the folly of rewarding A, while hoping for B. *Academy of Management Executive*, **9**, 7–14.

Peterson, D. B., & Hicks, M. D. (1995). *Development first: Strategies for self-development*. Minneapolis, MN: Personnel Decisions International.

Shaw, K. N. (2004). Changing the goal-setting process at Microsoft. *Academy of Management Executive*, **18**, 139–42.

Chapter 16

High Potential Programs

The Challenge

You know you have bright, talented individuals who could be your organization's future senior leaders, but you're not sure how to identify them. Perhaps you worry that identifying any one group of individuals as "high potential" will disenfranchise those not identified, but you know you can't take the risk of not developing your next generation of leaders. Developing and supporting individuals who might one day be leading your organization is key to accomplishing your business strategy. The good news is that investing in high potential programs does pay off. The challenge is where to begin. And, if you have a high potential program, what can you do to make it better?

The Bottom Line

Don't Wait

To develop a robust leadership pipeline, start looking at people early in their careers in relation to your business strategy, asking "Do they have the capacity to drive the future business?" Sometimes organizations wait for individuals to prove themselves rather than challenging and supporting leaders early in their careers. Be conscious about the assignments and experiences offered to young leaders. Use the guidelines provided in earlier chapters to structure early work experiences to achieve maximum benefit for the business and the individuals who rise to the challenge.

Be Rigorous and Flexible

Force yourself to identify and communicate criteria that will differentiate top performers with growth potential and invest in developing these leaders. Know that the criteria for identifying "high potentials" will continue to evolve as will the individuals. Factors related to leadership ability, personal development orientation, mastering complexity, and culture fit will always be important for senior leaders in an organization.[1] However, make sure you also keep the high potential list fluid with people added and dropped as the organization's needs vary and change. People need to know that the list of high potentials is flexible. It shouldn't be a "free ticket" into senior management, and falling off the list shouldn't be permanently fatal. The truth is that organizations are poor judges of who will be senior executive material in 10 years: People and organizations change too much. Your high potential list should reflect this reality.[2]

Make the High Potential Program One Part of Your Overall Leadership Development Strategy

Make sure all leaders in the organization are provided several ideas about how they can develop themselves. The experiences, competencies, and relationships that you identified in Part I of this book should provide an abundance of ways in which leaders can stretch themselves right where they are. The truth is that those stretch experiences are likely to be more powerful than anything you can do in a high potential program.

Leverage High Potentials

Invest as much in developing this group of individuals as you do in identifying them.[3] Ensure that individuals identified as high potential are given learning and development opportunities that also further the business. For example, view them as a resource pool that could address significant business challenges or identify opportunities for future business growth.

Focus on Action Learning

High potential programs should be fully integrated with what leaders are learning and being challenged to do in their current jobs. The program should complement and accelerate their experience-based learning. Henry Mintzberg at McGill University in Montreal has noted that most MBA programs teach people the science of management, but fail to teach managers the practice of management.[4] High potential programs should expose high potential leaders to new perspectives (e.g., exposure to senior executives), leveraging the development strategies discussed in this book (e.g., stretch assignments, mentoring, networking, reflection) to accelerate the leaders' development. Good management development programs force managers to wonder, probe, struggle, analyze, synthesize, and integrate what they are experiencing. See chapter 18 for more ideas about how you can build your high potential program on experience-based development.

Taking Action

Define Selection Criteria

What does "high potential" mean for your organization? Most organizations tend to equate performance results with potential because performance is perceived to be "objective." But performance only tells part of the story; that is, it is necessary but not sufficient. You also need to take into account how the results were achieved. Are your top performers your role model leaders? Do they consistently demonstrate integrity? Are they developing others? The future success of your business rests equally on these dimensions that are more difficult to assess. Furthermore, performance isn't always as objective as we would like. Leaders can get short-term results and cripple an organization while they do it. Their performance also depends on the businesses they lead. Leaders of business units in growth markets will contribute more bottom line revenue than leaders in sustaining businesses. So don't only look at the strongest businesses, but take advantage of organizational setbacks and crises to spot high potential individuals who may have been overlooked during good times. Comparing bottom-line results without taking the organizational context into account could encourage a culture of mediocrity – why step outside of my comfort zone if I am just going to be penalized for it?

When evaluating leaders, consider both their performance and their future potential. It is important to define performance and potential in a way that is meaningful and relevant to *your* business (see Figure 16.1 to see how you can assess them as two separate dimensions). The box below provides an example of the kinds of criteria you can use to assess potential in your organization.[5] Force yourself to consider competencies that will drive your future business performance.

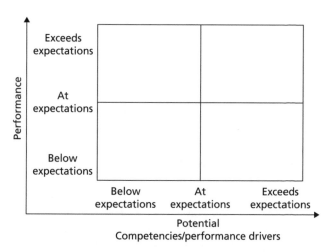

Figure 16.1 High potential identification matrix

Example:
High Potential Identification Criteria

Individual Capabilities

Use your competency model, especially those competencies related to:

- Propensity to lead (steps up to take charge and leads by example)
- Brings out the best in people (creates energy)
- Authenticity (genuineness, honesty, integrity)
- Openness to feedback (is open to and actively seeks feedback)
- Learning agility (constantly reinventing themselves, looking to improve, and applying lessons learned to future challenges)
- Adaptability (juggles competing demands, "can do" attitude in face of change)
- Conceptual thinking (broad, big picture thinking)
- Navigates ambiguity
- Culture fit ("walks the talk")
- Results-oriented (gets things done, tenacity, perseverance)

Personal Aspirations

Consider the following personal aspirations to identify high potential leaders:

- Drive for growth (seeks diverse developmental experiences, takes risk to grow skills and abilities)
- Ambition (seeks out larger roles with more impact and responsibility)
- Mobility (willing to relocate)
- Alignment (sees the company as a good place to advance their career)

Organization Context

Consider your organization's pressure points and look for potential to emerge:

- Building new businesses or creating new products
- Operating in emerging markets
- Underperforming and overperforming business areas
- Crisis situations (e.g., workforce downsizing, unpredictable environmental disasters, sudden senior management departures)
- Exposure to external constituencies (e.g., media, regulatory agencies, governments, legal entities)

Be Transparent

Ensure that decisions regarding the identification and development of high potentials are taken early and communicated appropriately across the organization. For example, how will the selection criteria be disseminated throughout the organization? How will individuals be notified of their inclusion in the high potential pool? How will the high potential pool balance stability and fluidity such that individuals can enter and leave and re-enter as appropriate?

Be Explicit About Expectations

It is important that expectations associated with participation in a high potential program are clarified from both an individual and organizational perspective. Being part of a high potential program is not a guarantee for promotion or advancement. The organization will invest in the development of high potential individuals, tailoring learning and development opportunities to individuals in the high potential pool, but it is expected that high potentials engage in the development opportunities offered to them. It may be important to clarify expectations regarding travel and mobility and the amount of time individuals will be expected to invest in the program outside of their regular jobs.

Focus on Development

Design a program for high potential development to ensure appropriate benefits for individuals and for the organization. See the sample High Potential Development Checklist below. Development objectives should include increasing individual self-awareness, enhancing leadership capabilities, building an internal network, understanding the business strategy and its value chain (including increased knowledge of products and clients), and increasing awareness of the external environment. Ensure that senior role models in the organization, those connected to the future business strategy, get to know high potential individuals and are involved in regular reviews of them.

Example:
High Potential Development Program Checklist

☐ Focuses on experience-based development more than traditional training
☐ Incorporates opportunities to address real business challenges
☐ Involves senior leaders (as instructors, discussion leaders, coaches, mentors)
☐ Fosters the application of peer coaching and mentoring opportunities
☐ Focuses on increasing visibility of high potentials
☐ Includes effective and frequent development and career planning conversations
☐ Takes individual career aspirations into account
☐ Broadens individuals' perspective of opportunities in the organization
☐ Introduces thought leaders from outside of industry
☐ Emphasizes reflection as key mechanism for learning
☐ Provides opportunities to give and receive feedback (from peers, colleagues, managers, externals)
☐ Builds accountability for increased self-awareness (strengths, weaknesses, ambitions, values)
☐ Highlights the culture of the organization

Clarify Metrics and Outcomes

Understand that the goals and objectives underpinning a high potential program will impact its design and implementation. Proactively consider a balanced scorecard of metrics in relation to the success of any high potential program. If you focus on a single metric, you run the risk of simply selecting individuals based on this objective, possibly losing sight of those with real potential. For example, if a primary objective of your high potential program is related to increased retention, your selection criteria might target those at risk of leaving the organization. Consider a range of metrics and objectives, such as retention, promotion rate, diversity, and mobility. This will lead to a broader, more diverse high potential population.

To Learn More

The following books and articles provide more information about identifying and developing high potential individuals within your organization.

Byham, W. C., Smith, A. B., & Paese, M. J. (2002). *Grow your own leaders: How to identify, develop, and retain leadership talent.* Upper Saddle River, NJ: Development Dimensions International Inc. & Prentice-Hall, Inc.

Conger, J. A., & Fulmer, R. M. (2003). Developing your leadership pipeline. *Harvard Business Review,* **81**(12), 76–84.

Mintzberg, H. (2004). *Managers not MBAs: A hard look at the soft practice of managing and management development.* San Francisco: Berrett-Koehler.

Chapter 17

Succession Management

The Challenge

You think your organization does a pretty good job planning for job replacements, but you wonder if you're doing enough to develop leaders for future challenges. Perhaps you have noted consistent capability gaps among your succession candidates or you worry that the identified successors aren't diverse enough in terms of strengths, organizational knowledge, or basic demographics. Or maybe you feel confident filling senior level vacancies but are uncertain how to identify the "next" assignments for more junior leaders in your organization.

If you have these or other worries related to succession management, you are not alone. The changing demographic poses a significant challenge for all organizations. About one in five senior executives from Fortune 500 companies are eligible for retirement right now. In the US alone it is estimated that 30 percent of the population will be over the age of 55 by 2020.[1] Further, in economic downturns organizations can lose significant numbers of talented individuals. Hiring talent from outside the organization will get even more difficult, making the lack of internal bench strength all the more apparent.[2]

Traditional succession planning methods focused on building a list of successors who could fill senior leadership vacancies in the organization. These methods are insufficient to address today's challenges. A more holistic and comprehensive framework for succession management is required.[3] This chapter focuses primarily on what large organizations can do to address these challenges. However, most of the ideas and tools offered are equally applicable to small companies where succession issues are less complex in some ways (albeit more complicated in other ways where the previous owner or family has greater influence).[4]

The Bottom Line

Be Proactive and Strategic

In essence, succession management is about (1) anticipating the future needs of the organization based on its business strategy; and (2) finding, assessing, developing, and monitoring the "human capital" required to make this happen. In this strategic context, there are immediate implications. For example, don't wait for an individual to vacate a pivotal role in the company that could serve as an ideal development opportunity for someone else. Look deep into your leadership pipeline to analyze experiences, competencies, and relationships. Don't wait for gaps or inappropriate trends to emerge at the senior management level (e.g., poor performance, weaknesses in specific competency areas, or inappropriate diversity in terms of background, experiences, capabilities, demographics). Succession management is an ongoing process.

It Can't Be Delegated

One of the most important roles of the CEO is to own and manage the succession management process. Companies cannot have effective succession management systems without senior level endorsement, support, and involvement.[5] Ensure succession drives and is driven by the overall business strategy. Line executives are much more likely to embrace succession management when it reinforces business goals and objectives as opposed to being regarded as a separate system focused on human capital. Senior managers, not HR, should own the program. If the identification and development of the next generation of leaders is viewed as an HR exercise, run by HR for HR, it will not be considered meaningful to the business. The process has to be defined and owned by senior managers who will make role change and promotion decisions.

Succession Management Can't Happen in a Vacuum

Any succession management process that occurs in isolation from other organizational systems is weakened. Effective succession management requires rigor in key HR systems such as performance management and workforce planning, and flexibility in others such as compensation and benefits and relocation. (See Table 17.1 on page 158 for a checklist of some of the key systems and processes that need to support succession management.)

Taking Action

Ensure That Leaders are Developing Future Leaders

Build a culture that encourages leaders to identify potential successors and ensures they are ready to assume their role. Don't let them get stuck in their present role because they haven't developed a successor. Leaders should be responsible for developing the people on their team to assume a variety of roles inside and outside of the department. And senior executive committees will always be responsible for staffing senior positions (i.e., this is not the responsibility of current incumbents). One way to address what may seem like competing goals is to incorporate "employee development" in your performance management system as a criterion to identify and reward your best leaders. (See Chapter 15 for indicators you can use to identify and reward employee development.)

Identify Key Positions, Individual Aspirations, Capabilities, and Gaps

Begin with an understanding of critical roles within the organization and marry this with a thorough understanding of individuals' aspirations, experiences, competencies, and relationships. Don't think about replacing an individual, or filling a role; rather, consider building a pool of individuals to assume and develop in pivotal jobs for the future.[6]

Critical roles. Start with the business strategy when identifying key organizational roles: What kind of work needs to happen in order to accomplish your strategy? This is a useful activity no matter where you are in the organization.[7] For example, some of your critical roles

Table 17.1 Systems and processes that influence and are influenced by succession management

HR process	Key questions
Workforce planning	• How many senior leader positions do we have in our business? How many of these are considered "critical positions"? • How will this change over the next five years in response to forecast changes in business? • Who was promoted, advanced, or changed jobs last year? • What proportion of first-, middle- and senior-level leadership roles are occupied by people from diverse backgrounds (e.g., gender, race, geographical location, culture)? • What percentage of our workforce (employee, first-, mid-, and senior-level) is over 50 and 55 years of age? • How many senior leadership vacancies do we expect? • What is the net inflow and outflow of staff for the business/region as a whole?
Compensation	• To what extent do compensation practices limit mobility across businesses or regions? • Who are the most highly compensated leaders?
Relocation/ internal transfers	• What percentage of individuals transferred into or out of the business last year? • How many individuals are on short-term assignments? • What is the profile of the people who leave?
Diversity	• What are the overall workforce demographics? • What are the demographics of the high potential pool in my business/region? Is it representative?
Performance management	• What are the percentages of employees/leaders with annual performance goals? With development plans? • What percentage are having end-of-year and ongoing feedback discussions? • What is the quality of the feedback discussions they are having?
Leadership development	• What is the status of actions resulting from previous talent and succession reviews? • What are the trends (strengths, gaps) in the leadership population? How do these differ by leadership level? • What is the success rate of individuals who moved into new roles last year?

will be in regions or countries or product lines that you expect will grow in the coming years. Use the experience, competency, and relationship taxonomies you created in chapters 1–3 to help identify the positions that will best develop future leaders. Other criteria for homing in on critical roles might include:

- *Direct revenue produced*: What businesses/products/sectors are responsible for the most direct revenue contribution?
- *Customer–client interaction*: Which areas of your organization have the highest level of direct customer–client interaction? What roles might be interfacing deeply with the customer–client groups that are critical to your future strategy?
- *Unique skill set*: Which roles require specialized skills? What roles have been difficult to fill lately (due to lack of skills)?
- *Critical to core business*: Which roles drive your core business(es)?

Individual aspirations. Ensure that your succession management approach doesn't overlook or underestimate an individual's personal career goals and aspirations. Creating a match between the organization's future needs and the aspirations of individuals is the "magic" behind truly effective systems. The only way to keep talented people is to provide them with growth opportunities that challenge and stretch them in more promising ways than what the competition might be offering. Factoring individual aspirations into succession processes requires a culture that encourages ongoing conversations between leaders in your organization and tangible follow-through. What roles is the individual really interested in? Does the individual aspire to broad, general management responsibilities, or is the person focused on becoming a top notch technical specialist? Would an assignment outside of his or her home country be viewed as a positive opportunity or paying one's dues or completely unrealistic? Is the individual interested in developing new skills sets, or expanding existing expertise in other product or functional areas?

Experiences, competencies, and relationships. Use the key experiences, competencies, and relationships that you identified in chapters 1–3 to assess individuals' strengths and gaps. For each person, highlight key differentiators as well as areas for development. See the box below for an example development plan coming out of a rigorous succession management process.

Example:
Succession Management Template

Name of High Potential	**Current Position and Title**	**Time in Position:**
Pat Smith	Senior Vice President European Operations	2.5 years **Tenure in Organization:** 10 years **Previous Roles:** Vice President Risk Management (global role) Director US Operations Technology Director US Manufacturing Operations

Performance Summary

Exceeded expectations on number of risk mitigation and turnaround projects resulting in significant cost savings and protection against loss due to faulty operations. Restructured and streamlined organization resulting in more effective staff utilization.

Key Experiences	**Relationships**	**Competency Strengths**
Managing problem employees Turning projects around Profit and loss accountability	Internal with legal, compliance, audit, business heads	Problem solving and innovation Performance Teamwork Communication

Possible Next Roles

Role with direct accountability for establishing and managing customer relationships to enhance client focus capabilities.

Experience with labor relations and/or government entities to extend Pat's demonstrated ability to build solid internal relationships and test strategic, big-picture problem-solving capabilities.

Ready-Now Roles

Senior Vice President Compliance and Audit, Head of Manufacturing Operations for Core Business, Head of India Operations.

Ready 1–3 Years

President Global Operations, Chief of Staff.

Conduct (at Least) an Annual Organizational Review

One of the most basic and essential recommendations is to schedule an annual succession management review well in advance. The meeting requires time investment and participation from senior executive committee members, and scheduling these meetings at least one or two years in advance is a requirement. In the case of board level involvement for executive committee succession discussions, schedule the meetings as much as three to five years in advance. The essential items that should be addressed during these annual reviews are illustrated in Figure 17.1. A typical meeting agenda is provided in the box below.

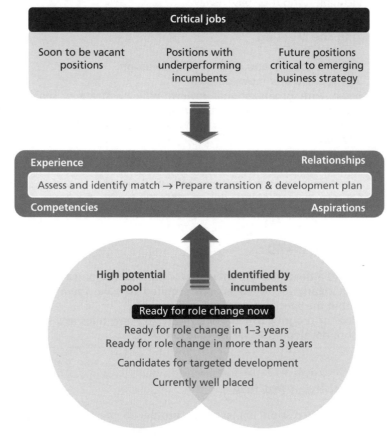

Figure 17.1 The succession management process

Succession Management Meetings Guidelines

Before the Meeting

☐ Prepare a description of each critical role based on current operating plan and business strategy.
☐ Prepare profiles of current role incumbents highlighting: performance, aspirations, experiences, competencies, and relationships.
☐ Identify "feeder pool" successors who can be ready to fill the role immediately, within one to three years, more than three years. The feeder pool comprises the high potential population and previously identified succession candidates (based on incumbent input or past reviews).

During the Meeting

☐ CEO sets context and leads candid discussion.
☐ Stay focused and move quickly.
☐ Begin with organizational review: business strategy, senior executive positions, and critical roles.
☐ Review high level summary of actions following last year's review.
☐ People review begins with current incumbents to critical roles followed by feeder pool discussion: ready for role change, targeted development in existing role, well-placed.
☐ Capture salient points during discussion with feedback to respective businesses and HR systems.

After the Meeting

☐ Create a development template for each succession candidate with clearly identified actions required to have them ready within the specified timeline.
☐ Monitor progress of individuals assuming new roles as well as those developing towards "ready now."

Be Creative and Practical

Make your succession management process so practical that line managers want to use it. Keep things simple without losing quality.

Technology can support effective succession management processes but don't rely on a system at the expense of content. Focus on catalyzing quality discussions among senior leaders.

Discussions in the meetings should center on practical issues – on the work that needs to be done currently and in the future. Consider combining existing roles to expand breadth or depth of accountabilities. In cases of high potentials ready for role changes, consider creating new roles that would leverage their strengths and develop them in new areas. Ensure that existing compensation processes don't impede movement across business units or geographical boundaries. Consider secondary roles outside of your organization, for example, in a customer/supplier organization or governmental body, to enhance capabilities of a member of your high potential pool.

Develop Tomorrow's Leaders

We return to where we began the chapter: Succession management is about (1) anticipating the future needs of the organization based on its business strategy; and (2) finding, assessing, developing, and monitoring the "human capital" required to make this happen. It's hard work, but the alternative is to rely on "survival of the fittest" to identify your future leaders. Unfortunately, tomorrow's challenges won't be the same ones that leaders survive today. The time you invest in growing future leaders is an investment in the current and future strength of your organization.

To Learn More

The following books and articles provide additional guidance and tips in the development of effective succession management systems.

Bower, J. L. (2007). Solve the succession crisis by growing inside-outside leaders. *Harvard Business Review*, **85(11)**, 91–6.

Corporate Leadership Council (2007). *Executive summary – high impact succession management: From succession planning to strategic executive talent management*. Washington, DC: Corporate Executive Board.

Karaevli, A., & Hall, D. T. (2003). Growing leaders for turbulent times: Is succession planning up to the challenge? *Organizational Dynamics*, **32**, 62–79.

Rothwell, W. J. (2005). *Effective succession planning: Ensuring leadership continuity and building talent from within*, 3rd edn. New York: AMACOM.

Chapter 18

Leadership Training Programs

The Challenge

Leadership training programs can (and do) play an important role in the development of leaders. For example, they are a great way to introduce complex models and new ideas in your organization. They can offer a safe haven for leaders to try out new skills. They are also a great place for leaders to get away from the daily demands, reflect on strategic issues, and connect with others to share best practices.

However, building leadership development programs that trigger real change is hard work. The barriers are formidable. Changing the way leaders see the world and helping them to approach problems in new ways is not easy. The status quo is the status quo for a reason – because it has been successful in the past. It takes work for people to change and even more work to change the culture. Even getting leaders to attend training programs can be difficult. Leaders will always have competing priorities and never enough time. Moreover, leaders face daunting obstacles after the training when they return to their jobs. They likely return to full email inboxes, new crises that have emerged, a backlog of decisions that need to be made, and a natural attraction to the status quo. The fact that leadership programs result in any change (and the research says that they do)[1] is rather surprising.

The best development programs are closely aligned with the business strategy, draw on leaders' previous and current experience, challenge leaders to work on real problems, and serve as a catalyst for on-the-job development beyond the program. In this chapter, we will discuss what line leaders, HR leaders, and training professionals can do to build programs that drive real change in the organization.

The Bottom Line

Start with the Business Strategy

The impetus for your leadership development program could start anywhere. Senior leaders sometimes have been known to launch new training programs based on the latest management fad or a great leadership program they just attended (e.g., wilderness training, business school). Training and development professionals are equally susceptible to trends. New training methods (e.g., web-based training) or new interpersonal skills training programs (e.g., emotional intelligence) tend to be their Achilles' heels. Starting with the business strategy will help ensure that the training program content and results are linked to things that matter, and ultimately the organization's bottom line. Even if training is outsourced, it is critical for a respected internal person to work closely with the external supplier to ensure that the program delivered directly supports the business and is relevant.

Aligning training with the business strategy helps ensure that new ways of thinking and new skills are more likely to be supported and reinforced by the organization. Leaders should be able to practice and use the new skills on the job, and the new skills are more likely to be rewarded because they are consistent with the company direction. It will never be perfect. There will be resistance. Change will be slow. The key point to remember is that training is more likely to have a positive impact when it is aligned with the business strategy.

Make Sure it's a Problem that Training Can Solve

Training is often the first, and sometimes the only, "solution" considered. Unfortunately the root problem may be something else – the reward system, how people are held accountable, a lack of resources, poor hiring practices – that is not solvable by training. Before treating the symptom, every potential training program should start with an organizational needs analysis to understand what the problem really is, identify root causes, and what role, if any, training can play in solving it. If training *is* part of the answer, the organizational analysis will also identify actions necessary to support the change. The needs analysis should include:

- Discussions with key people in the company who understand the complexity of the issues
- A best-practices analysis to find out how other organizations have dealt with the problem and lessons learned
- A review of the research on the topic to identify what works and what doesn't
- Conversations with the leaders actually doing the work to understand their pain points and how the training program can directly address their needs.

And remember, sometimes, when all is said and done, it might just turn out that training isn't the answer!

Form a Partnership Between Line Management and HR

Senior line leaders and training professionals both bring valuable insights and skills to the table. Line leaders bring their knowledge of the business – where it is and where it needs to go. Training and HR professionals bring their expertise in learning methodologies and how training can be structured to maximize its effectiveness. Working together, they can build a robust developmental experience that will result in real change. They can join forces to define the expected outcomes, the targeted audience, the content, and how the training should be delivered. Leadership programs naturally engender more credibility and respect when they are "owned" by senior leaders rather than HR. Recognizing this, it is equally critical that senior leaders work with HR and training professionals to ensure that programs are based on solid learning principles. For example, 50 years of research suggests that lecture isn't the best learning modality to teach things like complex problem solving or developing new skills (which are the goals of most leadership programs). A partnership between line leaders and HR can focus the training on the right topics using the right methods to teach it.

Focus on Action Learning

Training is most effective when leaders are required to work on real problems that they are facing in their jobs. The reasons are obvious: they are working on problems they care about, they are practicing the new skills that they need to develop, and they are working on real business challenges and generating real solutions that they can directly apply.

There are many ways to build action learning into training programs.[2] In some programs, senior leaders identify the business issues that training participants will work on during the program, and request that participants present recommendations to them at the end of the program. In other programs, participants are asked to bring their own business challenges, and these challenges become case studies that are worked on throughout the training program. For example, leaders apply new strategy models, marketing techniques, and finance metrics to a product or service they own during the training session. Still other programs might use business simulations that require participants to learn and practice new skills. Less robust programs might use hypothetical case studies or ask participants to discuss specific examples in their business that are related to concepts introduced in the training program. The key point to remember is that the more the training program challenges leaders to focus on their actual work, the more likely leaders will be to use the content in their jobs.

Taking Action

Develop Yourself

There are a variety of things you can do to ensure that you are getting the most out of leadership development programs that you attend. Before you go, identify your personal goals for the time there. During the sessions, capture any actions you want to bring back. Consider how you will apply what you have learned into your day-to-day life. Connect with other people and draw on their experience. The truth is you may learn more from them than from any of the speakers. Remember what a great opportunity it is to unplug from the daily grind and reflect on some of the bigger issues in your work. When you get back, take 15–30 minutes to review your notes, identify the key ideas, and build them into your job. Find ways to use the new ideas within the first month. Try not to add any extra tasks to your job but find ways to use the information to approach old problems in new ways. Share the key learning at your next staff meeting, both to reinforce the information in your own mind and so your direct reports can benefit from what you learned. Be a role model in your own commitment to continuous learning.

Develop Your Team

Don't be the manager who puts attending the organization's leadership development program off until the last possible moment because you always have more important things to do. After all, this is probably a good test of your leadership: Have you developed a team that is strong enough to function without you? When your team members go to training, support the application of the training concepts back on the job. Research suggests that management support is a strong predictor of whether or not the content from the training will get used.[3] Before a training session, talk with your team members about what they hope to bring back. Challenge them to think about the training in relation to their work and their broader career goals. Make time during team staff meetings for them to share lessons learned. Again, this doesn't have to be something extra. You might add a standing section to team staff meetings called "lessons learned," when all team members report leadership lessons they have learned in the past week. In the following weeks, check in and see if they are still applying what they brought back.

Build Leadership Development Programs into the DNA of the Organization

Line leaders and training professionals both play critical roles in the success of leadership development programs. An example of how this partnership might work in practice is provided in the case scenario below.

Case Scenario:
Designing a Leadership Development Program

AKA, Inc. has a well established and successful product line that will need to be updated soon. A new CEO was hired to drive the change and increase innovation. One of the action items on the CEO's plan is a training program on innovation.

In the following weeks, the company's training director meets with the CEO and says that he shares the CEO's sense of urgency but cautions that an off-target training program won't fix the problem, and will be costly. Worse, it could break something that is working. They agree that the first deliverable will be an organizational analysis to understand what's working and not working.

To begin, the director will interview senior leaders, two managers who have led teams that developed and successfully released new products in the last year, and a few first-level supervisors and employees in the company to assess the current condition. The director will also connect with people in three other comparable-sized companies who have successfully made recent advancements in their product strategies. Finally, the director will have someone in his department conduct a quick review of the research to identify the factors that predict new venture success and "intrepreneurial leadership" (successfully launching new products within an established company). The results will be presented to the senior management team in one month. The presentation will be a catalyst to discuss the key success factors for change, barriers in the company, and proposed next steps (including a leadership program design proposal if appropriate).

When the results were presented four weeks later, there was room for optimism. The entrepreneurial spirit that drove the company in the early years was still present, but as the company had matured, barriers had emerged that sometimes stopped new product innovations before they could gain momentum. The organizational systems had become so complex and interdependent that new ideas couldn't get off the ground. There were always five people to say no for every one who supported an idea. The reward system reinforced operational efficiency rather than innovation because things like cost-cutting could be more easily measured. There were few rewards for leaders willing to take calculated risks. Leaders tended to focus on fixing what was broken instead of exploring new possibilities. The director proposed that this last problem could be addressed in a leadership development program and was an important step in changing the culture. The senior leadership team agreed and gave the green light to develop the program. They also introduced several initiatives to begin addressing the other systemic issues.

A design team was formed that included the director of training, one of the senior managers who had successfully launched several new products in the past two years, a line supervisor with a track record for building highly innovative teams, an external expert specializing in new venture creation, and two training design experts from the training department. The senior leadership team was involved in modifying the content of the program. The two-and-a-half-day program was beta-tested with a small group of leaders recognized for their strong leadership skills who provided final content recommendations before the program was offered company-wide.

For the training, participants were required to bring a work-related example, a new product or service that they were currently developing. Throughout the program they were given new ways to think about their work (e.g., new venture financial models, how to select and execute an entry strategy, etc.) and opportunities to immediately apply the new ideas to their projects during working sessions. They were divided into peer groups and time was allocated for the groups to challenge and coach each other. Senior managers were responsible for facilitating the modules in their areas of expertise. A special two-hour module was included to identify the barriers they would face back on the job and strategies they could use to overcome resistance. At the end of each program, three of the proposals that were developed were selected and presented to the CEO. The presentations provided visibility for the products and a chance to elicit resources from senior leaders to launch the ideas. The CEO also used this as an opportunity to reinforce the value of innovation to the company's bottom line performance, reinforce other strategic priorities, and communicate her ongoing expectations. The training intervention included a six-month follow-up session for participants to present what they had accomplished since the class and share lessons learned along the way. Another member of the senior leadership team hosted these sessions so participants took them seriously.

To make sure participants came to the training prepared, emails were sent to participants and their managers encouraging them to meet together *before* the program to select the work projects that leaders should bring to the training program. In addition, before the program, participants were asked to conduct a mini-market analysis on their project and bring it with them. It was clear that the training program was going to be a working session.

Finally, evaluation systems were put in place to ensure the program was having the desired impact. Three months after the training, participants were contacted to determine how many of the projects were underway and how many had resulted in measurable results. Metrics were also tracked organization-wide to assess systemic changes, including the number of new products/services that were in the pipeline. The CEO and senior leadership team recognized that most new products/services would not hit the market for a year, but the early feedback was critical to ensure that the company was heading in the right direction and new innovations were moving through the early stages of the pipeline.

Senior line leaders. The leadership program should be "owned" and driven by the line, not by HR, if you want people to take it seriously. However, it's important that line leaders work in close partnership with training professionals to build a program that is robust and supports the future business strategy. Jointly develop the goals for the program and the measures you will use to assess its success. Use the leadership development program to introduce new initiatives and new ways to think about the business. Adopt a "leaders teaching leaders" philosophy and assign different senior leaders the responsibility for different modules in the program. Link them with training staff who can serve as consultants to ensure that the modules are based on solid learning principles. Actively participate in the program yourself. Use it as a way to communicate the messages you have for the organization and find out how people are responding to them. If the leadership development program is critical to the business, require everyone to participate. Send the program invitations from your office instead of from HR. Reserve the first sessions for senior leaders to emphasize how important the program is and so senior managers can support the changes in their organizations. Likewise, the location of the training program matters because it communicates how important the program is to senior management. This doesn't mean it has to be in an extravagant resort next to a golf course, but it should be a rich learning environment instead of a stale, sterile classroom. Several organizations have built corporate universities like GE's Crotenville Leadership Center to demonstrate the importance they place on leadership development.

Training professionals. As a training professional, the value you bring is your expertise in program design and delivery. You need to ensure the programs are built to promote learning and transfer beyond the classroom. Three things are especially important in your role: (1) stay connected to the business, (2) ensure that training interventions are built on solid learning principles, and (3) find ways to create a demand for the training program.

The first step is to stay connected to the business. Find opportunities to work closely with senior leaders; know what is keeping them up at night and how you can help. Equally important, stay connected with the people "on the floor" who do the real work, so you know what's really happening. Know the business strategy. Stay up to date on industry trends, read the corporate annual report and key internal communications, and know what external analysts are saying about your company. Understand the challenges that key business units in the organization are facing. Work with the recruiting and workforce groups in your organization to stay abreast of talent and skill gaps in the company. Be aware of new research and emerging trends in leadership development. Senior leaders need to be involved in defining the training program objectives, serving on an advisory board, and, ultimately, in the delivery of the program. Programs that don't have a senior line leader champion are doomed to fail.

Second, build every program on research-based training and development principles (see the "Basic Principles" box on page 175).

Finally, create demand for the training program. Program content is obviously important (e.g., providing leaders with skills they can directly apply in their jobs), but it is seldom enough. Leadership development programs are more likely to be viewed as valuable when they are "owned" by line leaders (not HR), when they require nomination by senior leaders, when space is limited, and when they are held in well-regarded locations (which could include corporate offices). Where appropriate, leadership training can be required or considered in promotion decisions (*if* there is evidence that the skills developed in the program are a business requirement). Leadership programs can also gain visibility when they are linked to ongoing initiatives. For example, imagine an organization that is adopting lean manufacturing practices in the coming year. A leadership development program might be required as a place for leaders to learn how to guide teams through the change process.

Make Sure Programs Offered by External Vendors Support the Business Strategy

More and more companies, large and small, are outsourcing their training to third-party vendors. However, all of the principles discussed above still apply. Any external provider needs to work within your business context with a strong commitment to deliver what you need. The best vendors are likely to say, "Here's what I do really well and here's how I might partner with you to meet your needs." They

Tips:
Basic Principles of an Effective Training Program

The following list represents some of the features to keep in mind as you develop any training intervention.[4]

Align with the business: Line managers and training professionals should work *in partnership* to identify program objectives, identify training needs, and finalize the content. Line leaders should participate in the training (as presenters and/or participants). The training program should ask leaders to bring and work through real business challenges they are facing. Training evaluation measures should be directly related to business metrics that the company cares about.

Use advanced organizers: People learn best when they are given a framework that they can use to organize and remember new information. Two things are particularly important at the beginning of the training program: (1) a visual model of how the information will be presented, and (2) the learning/performance objectives (i.e., what participants should know and be able to do by the end of training). Models can be used to visually capture how the concepts are inter-related. As the training program progresses, the framework and performance objectives should be referenced to help participants connect the new information to the larger context. Even simple cues like headings or notebook tabs can serve this function. At the end of the session, activities should challenge participants to review and integrate the information to identify higher level patterns and insights that cut across the topics.

Think "adult learning." Malcolm Knowles, a recognized expert in adult education, identified five characteristics that are especially important for adult learners: (1) Adults need to know *why* they are learning something; (2) adults want their learning to be *self-directed*; (3) adults bring more work-related *experiences* into the learning situation; (4) adults enter into a learning experience with a *problem-centered* approach to learning; and (5) adults are motivated to learn by *both intrinsic and extrinsic* motivators.[5] The most effective leadership training programs address all of these issues, helping leaders draw on past experiences, to solve real problems they are currently facing in their work.

Build networks: The truth is that the best training programs ensure that participants have the opportunity to discuss current dilemmas, share their insights, challenge one another, network, share best practices, and support each other. One of the key goals of any training intervention should be to create a space where people can learn from one another and build relationships that will endure and reinforce the concepts far beyond the classroom.

Require practice: The research is clear: Just listening to information almost never leads to significant behavior change. Repeatedly practicing a targeted behavior under varied conditions is significantly more likely to result in longer term behavior change. The most effective practice sessions include positive and negative examples, feedback, and problems that are as close to real life as possible.

Build in feedback: Practice without feedback is like throwing darts at a wall with your eyes closed. Without feedback, people will never learn what works and what doesn't and how to improve over time. The most effective feedback is frequent, contingent (includes information about why the performance was good/bad), and organized (includes an overall framework to help the recipient think about the feedback within a larger context/model). Some of the feedback dimensions particularly important in *interpersonal* communications are discussed in chapter 10.

Extend training over time: People learn and retain more when training programs are broken up into modules that are spread out over time. This, of course, isn't always possible when busy leaders need to be brought together in one location. Even in situations where the training is concentrated, requiring participants to do some preparation work before the program can lead to significantly more learning. For example, participants might be given questions to consider in advance of the session and asked to connect with three other participants to discuss their thoughts. Likewise, managers might be brought back together six months after the training session to discuss lessons learned, best practices, and new ideas.

Teach for transfer: The training program has failed if participants leave thinking, "That was great, but I can't apply any of it because my manager and the company won't support it." The training should directly address application issues. Challenge participants to identify and anticipate the barriers they will face, work through how they will respond, and review strategies that will build resilience (i.e., setting priorities, the power of small wins, avoiding self-blame, leveraging other people, and celebrating successes along the way).[6] Remember that the most effective training doesn't focus on content alone. The material is also a way for the participants to "learn how to learn." Imagine that only 10 percent of the learning takes place in the classroom and it is simply a catalyst for the rest of the learning that will occur later. How would you build a program if this were true?

Evaluate if it worked. Assess if the training actually led to behavior and performance changes after people have attended. If training programs were truly based on the business strategy, they should also impact the business metrics that are important in the company.

will recommend others if they aren't the best match. If they are a good match, establish their commitment to work in partnership with you. One final note, company leaders should always be an integral part of the leadership program in the ways discussed earlier, whether it is developed in-house or by an outside vendor.

To Learn More

Broad, M. L., & Newstrom, J. W. (1992). *Transfer of training: Action-packed strategies to ensure high payoff from training investments.* Reading, MA: Addison-Wesley Publishing Company, Inc.

Marquardt, M. J. (2004). *Optimizing the power of action learning: Solving problems and building leaders in real time.* Consulting Psychologists Press, Inc.

Mintzberg, H. (2004). *Managers not MBAs: A hard look at the soft practice of managing and management development.* San Francisco, CA: Berrett-Koehler.

Willmore, J. (2002). How to give 'em performance when they insist on training. *Training & Development Journal*, **56(5)**, 54–9.

Part V

Moving from Success to Significance

This book has focused on real time leadership development to improve leaders and enhance business results, but this ultimately raises an even larger question: *Leadership for the sake of what?*

We have worked with executives who, close to retirement or facing a plateau in their career, find themselves asking, "What now?" Throughout their careers, they have been driven by external measures of success, "Am I getting ahead and adding value? Did my team perform and hit their goals this year? Is my organization profitable? Is my business better now than it was when I took over?"

Leaders by nature are driven and competitive, if not with others, then with themselves. They want to do their best and get the best out of others. They hate to lose. This competitive drive is reinforced every day. There are lots of numbers to help leaders keep score, "How did I do against my goals? What was my salary increase/bonus this year? How does it compare with everybody else? Am I moving ahead in my career or am I stalling?" Sometimes the signals are so strong it's hard to step back and figure out what is most important. What's going to make a difference in the long run? There's always something that the leader should be doing and always another big challenge waiting. There's never enough time. It's so easy to lose sight of the big picture and even easier to lose track of oneself. Some leaders find themselves at the top of their career ladders, wondering in the quieter moments if the ladder has been leaning against the wrong wall.

We titled Part V "Moving from Success to Significance" because it captures the struggle that leaders feel. They want to be at their best, they want to succeed, and they want to live lives with purpose and meaning. There has been surprisingly little research conducted on these topics considering how important they are to most people. Leaders, more than any other group, need to be clear about who they are and where they stand. They play multiple roles and serve multiple constituencies both inside and outside of work. It is sometimes hard to figure out what is consistent, common, and most important across all these roles, and what is *most* important in the midst of ongoing and competing demands. In our work, we have had the opportunity to engage in deep conversations with a wide variety of leaders, across multiple industries, and in various career stages (e.g., new managers, senior executives, retired executives). We have asked these leaders to tell us how they ended up in a leadership role, the things that matter most in their lives, and how they define "success" in their lives and in their work. We have asked them to reflect back on their careers and tell us how their definitions of "success" have changed, if at all, over time.

As we talked with these leaders about their journeys, some consistent patterns emerged. Leaders often began their careers by focusing on their growth. They talked about being young, ambitious employees, eager to gain the experience they needed to get ahead, finding out what they were good at, and charting their future careers. They advanced up the management chain assuming new assignments and new challenges. Somewhere along the line, they inevitably hit a roadblock or found their career stalled. Maybe they repeatedly tried for a promotion that never happened, or consciously decided the price to get to the next level was just too high. At this point, many of these highly regarded leaders turned their attention from themselves and their own success to focus on the relationships in their lives, inside and outside of work. It was as if the leaders quietly said to themselves, "I'm not moving any more, but I can make a difference where I am. I can develop the people around me, and spend more time with my family." Some leaders found contentment at this stage, but some reached moments when these kinds of relationships weren't enough. Leaders had to make tough decisions that weren't popular and alienated some of the people who they cared about the most. Maybe a project fell apart and a senior leader or peer publicly placed the blame on them, and this became the story that everyone told. These were the times when leaders, independent of what anybody else thought, were forced to look in the mirror and figure out what they believed, what they were going to do, and the principles they would live by. This seems like a worthy destination for any leader, but several of the leaders we talked to, especially leaders toward the end of their careers, moved even beyond their personal principles to see themselves as one part of a very big picture. They moved to a place where they became catalysts, using their strengths and place in the world to release the potential in other people. They saw themselves as cocreators with the people around them. As leaders, their goal was to design organizations that could change and develop over time, and could serve as a place where others could flourish. Their vision was that, in time, new leaders could take the organization to places that the leaders themselves couldn't even begin to imagine. They focused on their legacy, but the legacy wasn't about their individual story; it was the privilege and responsibility to play a major or minor role in someone else's story.

In this spirit, the focus in this final section will change from leadership *development* to leadership *contribution* to discuss some of these larger life issues. We will concentrate on three areas that represent the places where leaders can and should wrestle with questions of purpose and meaning: (1) leadership transitions, (2) leadership principles, and (3) leadership legacies.

Chapter 19

Transitions

The Challenge

Transitions are a natural part of life in today's organizations. In the late 1980s, Peter Vaill described the challenges that managers face as "permanent white water,"[1] and it's only gotten crazier since then. Transitions can be intoxicating times of accelerated growth into new leadership levels. They can also be some of the most harrowing moments in your career, when you feel you have an equal likelihood of shining or failing gloriously. But transitions are more than just something to survive. Transitions always bring new possibilities. Think about the energy and perspectives that new employees bring to a team. They are the ones most likely to ask, "Why do we do it this way?" Organizations with leaders and employees who are used to making transitions are more likely to adapt to external changes as well. Accordingly, your challenge as a business leader or HR professional is to learn how to thrive in your own transitions and to help the leaders and employees in your organizations navigate the key transitions in their careers.

In this chapter, we will discuss the common types of transitions that leaders make, strategies that leaders and employees can use to successfully navigate these key transition points, and how senior leaders and HR professionals can build organizations that are agile and transition-friendly.

The Bottom Line

Transitions are the Rule, Not the Exception

We tend to think of transitions as a temporary state between times of stability; that is, we take for granted that stability is the norm and a transition is the exception. But what if transitions were the norm and stability was the exception? Tim Hall at Boston University suggests that this is exactly what is happening in the workplace today.[2] The average person today is likely to change jobs, companies, and even professions several times over the course of their careers. Hall suggests that careers increasingly have become person-driven rather than organization-driven. To succeed in this new reality, leaders and employees need a strong sense of *identity* (self-awareness, a sense of their strengths, and passion) and *adaptability* (the ability to learn, adapt, and build strong relationships). If transitions are the rule, then it is critical that all leaders, and all employees for that matter, to be aware of two things: (1) the typical kinds of transitions they will face in their development; and (2) strategies they can use to navigate through them successfully.

Typical Leadership Transitions

In their book, *Leadership Passages*, David Dotlich, James Noel, and Norman Walker identify nine common transitions that leaders face: joining a company, moving into a leadership role, accepting a stretch assignment, assuming responsibility for a business, dealing with a significant failure for which you are responsible, coping with a bad boss and competitive peers, losing your job or being passed over for a promotion, being part of an acquisition or merger, and living in a different culture.[3] All of these require different leadership skills. Promotions into higher management levels represent another set of key transitions that leaders face. Different management levels demand very different things of leaders. Ram Charan, Stephen Drotter, and James Noel identify six key leadership transitions in their book, *The Leadership Pipeline*: from managing yourself (as an individual contributor), to managing others, to managing managers, to functional management, to business management, to group management, to enterprise management.[4] Each stage presents new leadership challenges that require the leader to develop new competencies and new approaches, often requiring leaders to give up the very things that made them successful at the previous level. For example, new first-level managers need to stop seeing themselves as technical experts and start thinking about how they are going to manage and motivate the people who report to them.[5] Similar new demands occur at every level. The functional leader who is promoted to lead a business unit will have to move beyond seeing the world through his or her technical field (e.g., engineering), and learn how to draw on multiple disciplines (e.g., finance, human resources, operations, marketing) to drive the business as a whole.

These models and others remind us that leadership isn't a gradual increase in one's skills. It is more likely to be a series of wrenching nonlinear steps that require leaders to think, feel, and behave differently. Old strategies and old skills won't necessarily work in the new role and can sometimes even get in the way. Organizations are at their best when they help leaders anticipate the changes and navigate through them successfully.

Navigating Transitions Successfully

The types of transitions may vary widely, but the strategies to help you navigate through them remain largely the same. Here are some things to keep in mind as you approach your next transition.[6]

Identify what is required in the new role. Talk to people and read whatever you can about your new role before you move into the job. If you are changing companies, read analyst briefings, annual reports, and news stories in the popular press so you know the challenges facing the new organization. Identify the top priorities and key challenges in your new role. Find out what your new boss thinks about your team. Talk to your team – discover what they are proud of having accomplished in the previous year and what they think would move the team to the next level of excellence in the coming years. If this is a promotion, think about the kind of leadership that is required in the new role. Figure out what new skills are required and what you are going to have to give up.

Contract with your new boss how "success" will be measured. Meet with your new boss to identify what constitutes "success" in your new job and how it will be measured. Too many leaders pursue what they think is most important, only to find out later that their priorities weren't shared by their boss. Sometimes bosses aren't clear themselves. Sometimes they don't know exactly what they want. Sometimes the organization hasn't agreed on a direction, with different parts demanding different things. All of these are real possibilities but, at the end of the day, you will be held responsible for what you did or didn't accomplish, so clarify and manage these expectations from the beginning as much as possible.

Get to know your key stakeholders. Identify and meet with the people who will be critical to your success. Ask your new boss, peers, and team to help identify the key stakeholders. In the pressure to get some early wins – which are also important – building relationships with your key stakeholders may be one of the first tasks to fall off your priority list. However, talking to the right people from the start will help ensure that you are doing the *right* things. Ask them to discuss their perspective on: the key challenges facing the company, what your top priorities should be, the traps you should avoid, and their general advice for someone just starting in your role. Remember that if you start to derail in your new role, it will probably be something that other people see long before you do, so take the opportunity to ask them directly to give you feedback if they see you heading in the wrong direction. Keep the door open for future conversations.

Build a development plan. Execution will be your main focus in the first few months, but don't miss great learning opportunities along the way. Set aside time with your boss in the first couple of months to establish your development goals.

Look for small wins. Michael Watkins in his book *The First 90 Days* suggests that new leaders have three months to prove their value to the company in the new role.[7] That is the point at which their contributions should begin to outweigh their cost to the company. During the initial 90 days, it's important to log some early wins to establish your credibility and build momentum for later efforts. As a leader, most of your projects will stretch out for a year or more. Find ways to break them down so you have some deliverables and measurable results in the first three months.

Taking Action

Prepare for Your Own Transitions

Read one of the books listed at the end of this chapter so you can anticipate the challenges you will face and the strategies that are likely to lead to success. Before you get too busy doing the job, figure out what is really important. Use the Transition Checklist box to assess how you are doing.

Coach Your New Team Members Through Their Transitions

As a manager, you are one of the greatest factors in the success (or failure) of new people who join your team. Establish a high performance environment from the beginning with clear goals and a clear understanding of how "success" will be measured in their new role. As silly as it sounds, make sure the new person has the basics – a badge for the building, a key to their office, and a computer with email that works. Introduce them to the larger team. Walk them through a transition checklist (like the one provided in this chapter). Connect them with key stakeholders and other important people in their network. Help them identify some early small wins. Discuss their development goals for the year. Provide early, direct feedback if they start to wander off course or clash with the culture. Build a relationship that encourages questions.

Build a Transition-Friendly Organization

Use rigorous selection systems that are reliable and valid (e.g., structured interviews that have been validated) to select people who have the skills that they will need to succeed.[8] Build a culture where managers feel responsible and are held accountable for the success of new employees in their group. Introduce new employee orientation materials and programs if you don't have them already. Require that performance goals be established in the first 30 days of a new assignment

Your Transition Checklist

My Manager

I have met with my manager, and we have discussed:

☐ my manager's assessment of the team I am taking over;
☐ how "success" will be measured in this job (including the specific goals and deliverables that will be expected of me in the coming year);
☐ challenges and barriers that I am likely to face and my manager's ideas on how I might address them;
☐ key stakeholders who I should meet with;
☐ resources that I will need to be successful in this role;
☐ my development goals and long-term career aspirations.

My Direct Reports

☐ I have met with all of my direct reports to discuss the health of the team and the opportunities that they see to move it to the next level.
☐ I have met with each of them to discuss their performance goals, deliverables, and future career aspirations.

My Network

☐ I have identified the key people I will work with in this new role (senior leaders, thought leaders, peers, key people in other departments, customers, suppliers) and have scheduled meetings to meet with them within the first two months.
☐ I have identified the people I need to meet with regularly in this job and set up ongoing meetings with each of them.
☐ I have explicitly asked my boss, peers, and direct reports to give me feedback if they see me start to veer off course.

My Performance

☐ I have identified my top three priorities in this job.
☐ I have identified at least three small wins I will achieve in the first 30–90 days.
☐ I have documented my performance and development goals for the year.
☐ I have started to map out long-term performance goals for myself and the team.

and development goals in the first 60 days. Create a culture where it's common for people to move into new jobs or take on significant new responsibilities every two or three years. Encourage cross-training and job rotations. Make open jobs visible to everybody. Consider internal candidates first and establish a "promote from within" culture. Consider structuring your leadership development training around the key leadership transitions (e.g., first-time managers, new functional managers/executives, new business managers/executives) since these are the times when leaders can benefit from guidance the most. Provide special onboarding support for senior leaders joining the company (e.g., assigning a peer mentor, providing an internal coach, assigning them an experienced executive assistant who know the company well). Build a transition guide that all employees can access. Then monitor how you are doing by tracking six-month and one-year turnover rates (and other metrics – see chapter 4) for key jobs in the company.

To Learn More

Bradt, G., Check, J., & Pedraza, J. (2006). *The new leader's 100 day action plan: How to take charge, build your team, and get immediate results.* Hoboken, NJ: John Wiley & Sons.

Charan, R., Drotter, S., & Noel, J. L. (2001). *The leadership pipeline: How to build the leadership-powered company.* John Wiley & Sons.

Dotlich, J. L., Noel, J. L., & Walker, N. (2004). *Leadership passages: The personal and profession transitions that make or break a leader.* San Francisco, CA: Jossey-Bass.

Watkins, M. (2003). *The first 90 days: Critical success strategies for new leaders at all levels.* Boston: Harvard Business School Press.

Chapter 20

Leadership Principles

The Challenge

It can be easy to lose yourself in the daily crises and pressure that you face as a leader. In the midst of all the transitions and turmoil discussed in the last chapter, your leadership principles are one of the things that remain constant and provide stability.[1] In a world of change, you can't always control what's happening around you, but you can control who you are as a leader.

Living up to your own principles is a daily choice. Warren Buffet is said to have commented, "Somebody once said that in looking for people to hire, you should look for three qualities: integrity, intelligence, and energy. And if they don't have the first, the other two will kill you. You think about it; it's true. If you hire somebody without the first, you really want them to be dumb and lazy." As a leader, *who you are* is often as important as *what you do*. In this chapter, we'll discuss how you can identify and craft the principles that characterize your leadership, how you can challenge others to establish their principles, and how you build ethics and principles into your organization.

The Bottom Line

Some Principles Endure Across Time and Space

Some principles have endured the tests of time and translate across cultures. Research by Deanne Den Hartog and colleagues suggests that the leadership characteristics most valued in leaders are surprisingly consistent across the 62 cultures they studied.[2] The leaders that people valued the most were described as: trustworthy, just, honest, encouraging, motivational, confidence builders, dynamic, focused on excellence, decisive, intelligent, and win–win problem solvers. Other characteristics were also universally recognized as negative: dictatorial, a loner, noncooperative, ruthless, irritable, and nonexplicit. There are leadership characteristics that will always count – no matter where you are leading from. Spiritual faiths also offer several enduring principles like the Golden Rule ("Do unto others as you would have them do unto you") that have withstood the tests of time.

What Do You Stand For?

Some principles are so much a part of who you are that you couldn't articulate them if you tried, and if you did, they would sound like platitudes (e.g., be honest, treat people fairly). Other principles are more likely to be ones that you struggle with every day. They are the principles that you feel like you have to remind yourself to do every day. Some of them may sound like tired clichés to someone else, but cut to your very core (e.g., "I will put the company's goals before my department's goals." "I will always listen before I speak."). The principle might have come from a defining moment in your past. It may come from a past boss who did something you have committed to never doing as a leader. It may be that time you lost your temper. It may have come from a leader who you highly respect. Many leaders have shared examples of times when they lost sight of what they truly valued. One leader reflected that he gained many stamps in his passport, but lost his family in the process. Others reflected that they had missed significant events in the lives of their children (e.g., first steps;, sports tournaments, dance recitals, graduations) for the sake of key business functions. Later the important business deals are forgotten and they remember only the missed life event.

Taking Action

What Are Your Leadership Principles?

Use the questions in the "Finding Your Leadership Principles" box to start crafting your own leadership principles. Describe the kind of leader you want to be and the principles you want to live by. Consider the leaders you most admire and the characteristics that make them so significant in your life.[3] Think about the advice that you have received over the years that you will never forget.[4] Reflect on the readings and quotes that are particularly meaningful to you. Consider the beliefs and spiritual principles that are most important to you.[5] As you write your principles, have fun with them. Look for things you *want* to do, not the things that you feel like you *should* do. Write something radical that captures the passion that you feel. If, for example, you struggle with delegation, don't write that you will "delegate more effectively"; write something more drastic like, "If someone else can do this 75 percent as effectively as me, they should be doing it" to remind yourself that your job is not to do the work yourself but to empower other people. Some sample leadership principles are provided on p. 196. Yours, of course, will vary. Discover the principles that capture *your* convictions and passion.

Example:
Finding Your Leadership Principles

It is likely that you already have several leadership principles that define the way you lead. You may have never written them down. Use the following questions to reveal and craft your leadership principles. Remember that your goal is not only to identify the things that you feel you *should* do, but the principles that you *want* to live by. They need to capture your conviction and passion. They should have life. Find the ones that you want to be reminded of every day.

• Who were the most important leaders in your development? What were their leadership principles? What advice have they given you?
• What other advice have you received over the years that you will never forget?
• What do you struggle with every day in your leadership?
• What do you want other people to remember about you?
• If you come from a strong spiritual tradition, what captures the essence of this commitment for you?

Now put together 5–7 principles that capture the heart of what you have written down. Does it excite you? Would you be willing to ask others to hold you accountable to this list?

Hold Yourself Accountable

Post the principles where you can see them. Share them with other people and challenge them to hold you accountable so they are more than just words on a page. One leader we've worked with starts every new assignment by sharing his principles with his new team, as a way to establish his leadership style, and encouraging people to challenge him when he's not living up to his principles. Make them your principles first and not a list of platitudes you are imposing on others. Remember that who you are sometimes thunders so loudly that people can't hear what you say. To reinforce the principles, especially the ones that you struggle with, find readings (just 5–10 minutes) that will help you step out of the daily turmoil to focus on what's really important to you.

Example:
Leadership Principles

I will . . .
- always try to hire people who are more talented than I am
- remember that strategy is important, but in the end, execution is what really matters
- leverage my strengths and bring out the strengths in others
- always delegate a task if someone else can do it as effectively as me, and it will develop them
- always hold people accountable
- always speak the truth and create an environment where other people are willing to do the same
- do what I know is right regardless of the outcomes
- always listen before I talk
- remember that my family always comes before work, irrespective of the consequences
- always try to work myself out of a job and ultimately measure my success as a leader by what happens to the team when I am gone
- live by the Golden Rule in all that I do: "Do unto others as I would have them do unto me"; and sometimes that means taking actions and telling people things they don't want to hear
- always act like an owner (making decisions that are in the best interest of the company)

Challenge Your Team to Create Their Principles

Research suggests that your leadership is one of the most important predictors of ethical behavior in your team.[6] This includes both your personal role modeling and the work environment that you create. People tend to be much more ethical in environments where they have a trusting relationship with the manager and where they feel that they are being treated fairly. Personal integrity is the first step, but it's also important to expect the highest ethical standards of others. Work with your team to create a set of team principles that you will hold each other accountable to, or challenge team members to create and share their own leadership principles. Challenge them to share their principles with their direct reports.

Build a Principle-Driven Organization

In a review of the ethics research, Linda Treviño and colleagues at Pennsylvania State University, identified several characteristics that build a strong ethical culture in an organization.[7] The factors that appear to be most important include (1) a strong organizational culture that takes ethics seriously, and (2) a local workgroup climate that reinforces the message. This research suggests the company culture seems to be the most important. Relational cultures are related to higher ethical behavior while individualistic, competitive, organizational cultures appear to be especially dangerous.

Organizational processes that establish a strong ethical and principle-based culture include: an official code of ethics, an ethics hotline, mandatory ethics training, financial monitoring systems, sanctions and punishments for ethics breaches, and the elimination of reward systems that inadvertently reinforce unethical behaviors. Organizations where ethics are talked about tend to be more ethical. In the end, an ethical organization is one in which people make the right choices day after day. As a senior leader or HR professional, you by default are one of the standards that people measure themselves against. Living up to your ethical standards and principles doesn't guarantee that other people always will. Not living up to them almost always guarantees that other people won't either!

To Learn More

Badaracco, J. L. (1998). The discipline of building character. *Harvard Business Review*, **76(2)**, 114–24.

Covey, S. R. (1991). *Principle-centered leadership*. New York: Simon & Schuster.

McKenna, R. B., & Yost, P. R. (2004). The differentiated leader: Specific strategies for handling today's adverse situations. *Organizational Dynamics*, **33**, 292–306.

Quinn, R. E. (2005). Moments of greatness. *Harvard Business Review*, **83(7/8)**, 74–83.

Weaver, G. R., Treviño, L. K., & Agle, B. (2005). "Somebody I look up to": Ethical role models in organizations. *Organizational Dynamics*, **34**, 313–30.

Chapter 21

Legacies

The Challenge

As Benjamin Zander, Director of the Boston Philharmonic, has wryly noted, the conductor is the only person in the orchestra who doesn't make a sound.[1] The same is true for you – by definition, the only value that you add as a leader is through other people. Today, people are fond of referring to this as the leader's legacy. In this chapter, we'll discuss what a legacy looks like in a world of constant change. Your legacy begins with the strength of the organization that you build, but there is more. Your legacy is also captured in the relationships that you build, the principles that you live by, the potential that you release in others, and the life you live outside of work. Your legacy isn't defined by one moment in time, but by the hundreds of sparks that you kindle over the course of your life. This chapter challenges you to explore that legacy.

The Bottom Line

Build a Sustainable Organization

One of the ways to begin to discover your legacy is to ask yourself what you can do today that has a chance of still being around 10 or 20 years from now. The products and services that you offer today will likely be gone, but some things will remain. In your business, you might be able to define a strategy and market niche that could survive another 10 years. *Products and services* can be designed so they are differentiated from competitors in ways that protect the organization's position and prevent possible competitors from entering the market.[2] If you are in a support organization, you might put processes in place that could last that long. If you are a thought leader, you might create an innovation that changes the course of your profession for years to come. But legacy isn't limited to the business. The *culture* that you build could endure, if not in the larger organization, at least in the way the people in your group approach their work;[3] the time that you invest in your team members today could impact their careers for years to come. A strong *leadership pipeline* can have a profound and lasting change on the long-term success of the organization. All of these dimensions represent ways that leaders can have an impact that lasts beyond their time. As part of the succession planning process, one senior executive we worked with required every business unit to craft a document called "our story" that discussed the history, products, customers, future challenges, and key differentiators for the group. The story was posted at the top of the succession charts with the key positions and potential future leaders posted underneath to create a picture of the legacy they were attempting to create.

How Do You See Yourself as a Leader?

Psychologists have long noted that people continue to evolve and develop in predictable ways throughout their lives.[4] Robert Kegan, in his book *The Evolving Self*, suggests that there are at least five stages of adult development (see Table 21.1).[5] Some leaders are driven by personal needs (stage 2), others by the identification with and the approval of valued others (stage 3). Still others rely on and are driven by self-chosen principles (stage 4), and a few have progressed to see themselves as one player in a bigger picture, cocreating the future in partnership with others (stage 5). These stages affect how leaders see the world, how they behave, and how they define their legacy. Imagine the executive who is forced to choose between a promise to meet a customer's accelerated delivery schedule and the operations manager's insistence that it just can't be done. Stage 3 leaders are likely to spend a lot of sleepless nights trying to make the decision or defer to someone they respect. Stage 4 leaders are likely to fall back on their self-defined principles and take the actions they have decided are right. Stage 5 leaders are the least likely to take it personally, but

Table 21.1 Stages of Adult Development

Stage	Focus	Drivers
Stage 1: Impulsive	I am my impulses.	Impulses, perceptions
Stage 2: Imperial	I am my needs.	Needs, interests, desires
Stage 3: Interpersonal	You are my mirror.	Interpersonal relationships, mutuality
Stage 4: Institutional	I am.	Identity, principles, ideology
Stage 5: Interindividual	We are.	Interconnected relationships, an ever-changing self

instead consider the players and flow of events as one part in the company's story, and look for ways to bring people together to cocreate a solution. In all three situations, the final actions might be the same, but how they got there and where they found the "answers" will be profoundly different. Kegan suggests that most people today are in over their heads – in jobs that demand stage 4 thinking, while they are operating at stage 3. Struggling to stay afloat, these leaders look for someone else with the answer and are unable to separate themselves from the problem.[6] The dynamic and highly networked world of work today demands that leaders think at the more advanced levels. Unfortunately, moving from one stage to another is usually traumatic, compelling leaders to redefine and approach the world in completely new ways.

Think of Yourself as a Catalyst

You are one player in a very large system. Figure out the special role that only you can play. It may be a small role in a big play (e.g., a small but critical part in your company's future) or a big role in a small play (e.g., making your team successful). Consider how you can be the catalyst that brings people together and challenges them to cocreate the future. William Torbert calls this kind of leader an "alchemist."[7] These are leaders who want to build organizations and teams where people challenge and develop each other, and leverage each others' strengths. Catalysts look for small wins that can make a big difference; wins that will build allies and create momentum.[8]

Legacies and Life

It's important to always remember that your legacy extends far beyond the boundaries of work. You play multiple roles in your life. When they merge, they create conflict or possibilities. The widespread notion that work can be separated from the rest of your life is a fallacy. Who you are at work affects who you are at home and vice versa. Considerable attention in past years has been focused on reducing work–life conflict, but recent research suggests that trying to reduce conflict doesn't necessarily make people any more satisfied or productive.[9] Life and work are not zero sum games in which a gain in one area means a loss in another. The new research suggests that the better strategy is to look for ways that you can structure your life so the roles complement and support each other. Adopt a "both–and" mindset instead of an "either–or" mindset, acknowledging the different, yet important, contributions that each facet of your life can contribute to your overall satisfaction and success. Look for the ways that you can build legacies that bridge the many roles in your life.

Taking Action

Where Do You Find Your Value?

The author of Ecclesiastes could be any leader today when he cried in frustration over 2000 years ago, "Vanity of vanities; all is vanity" and "I hated all the things I had toiled for under the sun, because I must leave them to the one who comes after me. And who knows whether he will be a wise man or a fool? Yet he will have control over all the work into which I have poured my effort and skill under the sun."[10] Legacy is ultimately a question of where you find your value. This isn't just an intellectual exercise. If answered honestly, it likely goes to the very heart of who you are. *So, where do you find your value as a leader?* Take a few moments to reflect on the following questions: What if you never progress to a higher management level? Where do you find your value? What if, after you leave, your team falls apart? If you failed in your current job, where would you find your value? What if the people around you rightly or wrongly blamed you for the failure? What if you didn't live up to your own principles, what would be left? These can be terribly painful questions, but they are real questions that leaders somewhere are asking themselves right now. They are legacy questions.

Understand Your Working Leadership Model

Look over the stages of adult development in Table 21.1 and find where you fall. Consider how you think about your role as a leader. Then step back and consider what you do. Chances are, you often find yourself acting at a lower level. For example, you might tend to think at a systems level (stage 5), but the truth is that you find yourself constantly comparing how you are doing against other people (stage 3). Maybe you secretly experience a thrill of joy when you realize you have more money in your 401(k) savings account than the average person your age. Or maybe you find yourself comparing how your kids are doing versus other kids in their class at school. Maybe you can't sleep at night because you keep replaying a bad conversation you had with your manager. To really assess where you are, ask a few people who know you well (and will tell you the truth) to assess you. Ask them to provide some examples. Brainstorm some things you could do to practice leading at the next level.

Find Your Calling in the World

Finding your calling is the challenge to answer: "How is my work more than just a job?"[11] It is finding the place where you can use your strengths, passion, and purpose to make a difference. The writer and theologian Frederick Buechner defines this as "the place where your deep gladness and the world's deep hunger meet."[12] Drawing on this concept, part of your leadership legacy might be your ability to help your team members discover their strengths, develop their potential, and find their right places in the organization. At the organizational level, a calling shares some parallels with the "hedgehog principle" described by Jim Collins in his book *Good to Great*.[13] The companies that performed the best were the ones that knew the one thing they stood for (what they were passionate about, what they could do better than anyone else, and what drove their economic engine). Walk through the questions in the box below to consider your own calling. Better yet, ask a few close friends to answer the questions for you and see what they say. Think about your team members. What might be their calling? What might be your organization's calling?

Finding Your Calling

Set aside a couple of hours and find a place where you won't be distracted. Jot down your answers to the following questions. In the next few weeks, find a couple of people who know you well and ask them to give you input on the questions. Set aside time to consider all of the answers together. Write down the places inside and outside of work where the cluster of skills and interests that are unique to you differentiate you from the people around you. Find ways in the coming year that you can begin exploring these possibilities.

Strengths

- What comes particularly easy and quickly to you? What do you tend to do better than anyone else?
- What do other people say you're good at? What compliments do you consistently get that you discount and don't believe? What if they were true?

Passion

- Looking back over the jobs that you have had, what parts of your job(s) did you love to do? What did you hate?
- Imagine reliving your life. What are five imaginary jobs you would love to do? What do these jobs tell you about yourself?
- If you didn't have to earn a paycheck, what kind of work would you do? Are there elements that you can build into your current job? That you can build into your life outside of work?

Purpose

- Imagine yourself at your 80th birthday. What do you want people to say about you? What do you want to have accomplished?
- Consider the key roles in your life (e.g., family, work, community, spiritual, personal). What are your top three priorities in each area the coming year? Over the next five years?
- If you thought of your life as a series of mountains to climb, what would be most important right now in the journey?
- What purposes are trying to find you?
- If you thought you had a calling, what would it be?
- Maybe your calling isn't about what you do, but who you are. If this were true, what kind of person are you called to be?

Help Your Team Learn How to Play Jazz

In Western culture, we tend to think of organizations as big machines: getting the right parts in the right places at the right times, and making sure it is running efficiently. Today's organizations, however, are just as likely to be networks of people and departments inside and outside of the organization interacting to create products/services that customers want. A better analogy today might be to compare an organization with a jazz band. The power of jazz is that everyone is great on their own, but even better together. Jazz is dynamic, with different people taking the lead at different times, evolving and changing as they go. The whole is greater than the sum of the parts. Look at your team. How can you create an environment where people complement, enhance, and develop each other? How can you teach them how to play jazz?

Consider All *the Roles in Your Life*

Think about all the roles that are important in your life. Think of your life as a wheel. First, draw the "spokes" that are important in your life. These might include things like: work, family, health, friends, hobbies, spirituality, finances, and community. After identifying the dimensions that are important to you, place them around the wheel. Next, rate how satisfied you are with your life right now in each role on a scale from 1 (not content) to 5 (very content). Low scores should be plotted near the center of the wheel and high scores along the rim. Connect the dots. Then ask yourself some questions. What are your top three priorities in each of the roles in the next six months? What legacies do you want to build in each of the roles and across the roles? How would you like your wheel of life to look in six months? What are some of the hard choices that you are going to have to make? Rather than trying to reduce conflict between the roles, what are some ways that they can complement each other? What is the smallest step you could take today that would have the greatest effect in moving you closer to your goals? Return to this exercise once a month to remind yourself what is most important in your life.

Remember the Journey

Maybe your legacy changes over the course of your life and in the variety of roles that you play. Occasionally, you will find yourself in a job that you love doing, with work that is personally meaningful. At other times, you will just be trying to survive. And sometimes a job is just a job – a way to pay the bills and support your family. In the end, maybe your legacy isn't a mountain that you are climbing but a mountain range that you are exploring. Your job is to recognize those moments when you can make a difference, the flashes of legacy that emerge every day. These legacy moments may play out in ways you will never know. We all have people in our lives who will never know what they did for us. Maybe your legacy is to be that person for someone else.

To Learn More

Friedman, S. D., Christensen, P., & DeGroot, J. (1998). Work and life: The end of the zero-sum game. *Harvard Business Review*, **76(6)**, 119–29.

Kegan, R. (1982). *The evolving self: Problem and process in human development*. Cambridge, MA: Harvard University Press.

Palmer, P. (1999). *Let your life speak: Listening for the voice of vocation*. San Francisco, CA: Jossey-Bass.

Rooke, D., & Torbert, W. R. (2005). Seven transformations of leadership. *Harvard Business Review*, **83(4)**, 66–76.

Conclusion: The Bottom Line

The Challenge

We have covered a lot of ground in the book. Even though we warned you at the beginning that there was more than anyone could do, you may be feeling a bit overwhelmed or frustrated. You might be thinking, "Great ideas – but the truth is, I have a job to do!" We agree. A similar book could be written for almost every other part of your job as leader – strategy, marketing, finance, customer service, and operations management to name only a few. So, as we said in the beginning, give yourself the freedom to focus on the chapters and ideas that are most useful to *you*. Based on everything we have discussed in this book, we have identified below the seven most important things that *we* recommend that you do to develop yourself, your team, and your organization. Have fun!

For Your Development

1 *Find smart stretch assignments.* Throw yourself into experiences, assignments, and situations that will stretch you in the areas you have targeted for development. These can include weaknesses, untested areas, and strengths that you want to continue to build on. Almost any assignment can be a stretch assignment for someone. The secret is to find the ones that will challenge you in areas where you need to grow and make you more valuable to your organization.

2 *Write a development plan.* Just writing down your goals every year forces you to think about what is most important and helps you to see great stretch opportunities when they come your way. The best development goals are specific, challenging, measurable, and focused on on-the-job development.

3 *Create a feedback-rich environment.* Identify people inside your company (e.g., direct reports, peers, senior leaders) and people outside your company (e.g., customers, suppliers, professionals, friends/family) and invite them to give you feedback. Don't leave it to chance: ask them! Also find or build metrics that provide immediate feedback about how you are doing. The best feedback is immediate, frequent, and helps you understand *why* you did well or poorly.

4 *Get a mentor or coach.* Find someone who can coach and mentor you in your development. This should be someone who is further along in his or her career than you are and knows how to challenge you to grow in your career. It should be someone who you respect, who is committed to your success, and who is able to give you honest feedback.

5 *Perform.* Don't get so focused on future promotions that you underestimate the importance of your current job. The people who get noticed are the ones who do their jobs well. As we have noted throughout this book, the lessons of experience are learned on the job, so succeeding and capturing the lessons in today's job is the best way to prepare for tomorrow's opportunities.

6 *Focus on learning.* Take time to stop and reflect on what you are learning. One of the best ways to do this is to try to solve today's problems in ways that will also solve tomorrow's problems. Find ways to engage in real-time reflection: Conduct after-action reviews with your team, challenge yourself and others to build sustainable systems and processes in their work, analyze problems from multiple perspectives, and make sure you take time to reflect on your strengths and the weaknesses that consistently get in the way of your effectiveness.

7 *Remember that your job isn't everything.* All leaders plays multiple roles at work, in their family, with friends, and in their community. Leaders can sometimes let work define them. They start measuring their value by how well they are doing in their career. Identify your top three priorities in each of the roles in your life. Look

for ways to build a life where the different roles complement each other instead of competing. Set aside time every month to reflect on how you are doing.

For Your Team's Development

1 *Build a development plan with every team member.* Require all of your direct reports to write development plans every year. Reserve time on your calendar to meet with every employee and discuss their plans. Don't let it fall to the bottom of your to-do list.

2 *Focus on stretch assignments.* Don't just look for training classes, but find assignments that will give your team members a chance to stretch and grow. Look for assignments that are challenging and doable – where they have the skills to perform the job, but are challenged to grow in new ways. Look for some easy wins: Rotate team members between jobs, expand their scope and responsibility within a position, or give them a chance to work with new groups inside and outside the company that will broaden and stretch their perspective.

3 *Create a high performance culture.* Push leaders to be their best, to set challenging goals for their team, and execute against what they promised. Be careful what you reward. Promote leaders who are recognized for their effective performance and ability to develop strong teams.

4 *Create a feedback-rich environment.* Make sure that your team members build feedback systems into every goal so they can monitor and learn as they go along. The feedback should come from you *and* others *and* the work itself. Remember, the best feedback to other people is immediate, frequent, focuses on performance not the person, helps people understand *why* they did well or poorly, and looks toward the future.

5 *Connect your team to other people.* As a manager, you are likely to be the best person to link your direct reports to key people in the organization. Beyond helping people establish the connections they will need to get their immediate jobs done, you will also play an important role in helping them build relationships that will support their future career aspirations. This might include introductions to people in your network who can serve as mentors or assigning work

projects that allow employees to connect with other departments and opening future career paths.

6 *Build real time reflection into everybody's job.* At least twice during the year, ask employees to reflect on their progress against their development goals. Ask people to read a book or an article that will challenge the team to rethink how they are running the business, and discuss it at your staff meetings. In your one-on-one meetings, invite them to share the lessons they are learning about the business and themselves. Build milestones into projects to discuss what is working and what needs to change in the future.

7 *Think sustainability.* Consider your team five years from now. You probably won't be the leader. And it is almost certain they will be facing new challenges, requiring new skills and capabilities which are impossible for you to anticipate. So, what would it take for you to build a team that can change, grow, and adapt to meet that future successfully without you? Challenge your team members to ask themselves the same questions. Figure out, as a team, what you need to do to meet today's challenges in a way that will prepare you to meet tomorrow's challenges no matter what the future brings. Build continuous learning into everyone's jobs.

For Your Organization's Development

1 *Start with the business strategy.* Use the business strategy to identify the experiences, competencies, and relationships that are most critical in the development of future leaders. Use chapters 1–4 to help you get started.

2 *Build a rigorous performance management system and use it.* Require every employee to set performance goals for the year, create development goals for themselves, and then hold managers accountable for 100 percent completion rates. Separate the performance and development processes (and conversations) so managers are forced to focus on both. To be successful in today's dynamic markets, organizations need to execute against today's business goals *and* continuously improve to meet tomorrow's emerging challenges.

3 *Create a learning culture.* Create the expectation that people will stretch and grow, take on new responsibilities, and develop new skills. Remove barriers that prevent people from moving between different

parts of the organization. Challenge the organization to look at the business in new ways.

4 *Create a feedback-rich environment.* Create a culture where people are expected to give each other constructive and honest feedback. Feedback shouldn't simply focus on an employee's strengths and weaknesses, but focus on the person's potential.

5 *Focus on transitions.* Create a transition checklist that everyone can use to successfully navigate transitions in their careers (see chapter 19). Create guidance on how managers can support new team members. Focus special attention on the key transitions in your organization with programs to set people up for success (e.g., senior leader onboarding programs, new employee orientation programs, and development programs for leaders in key transitions).

6 *Build a principle-based organization.* Identify your leadership principles and ask your team to hold you accountable. Live by the principles you expect of others. Challenge your team members to build their own leadership principles. Build a strong ethics and principle-based culture. Create systems that reinforce and support the importance of ethics: a code of ethics, an anonymous ethics hotline, financial monitoring systems, strong and visible penalties for ethics breaches, and mandatory ethics training.

7 *Remember to focus on significance.* Think about your long-term goals and objectives. How can you create a sustainable organization that thrives and adapts to emerging challenges after you are gone? What do you need to put in place to create this type of organization? What do you want people to remember about you? Think of yourself as a catalyst, cocreating the future with the people around you.

Notes

Preface: Your Job is the Classroom!

1 See McCall, Lombardo, and Morrison (1988), McCauley, Ruderman, Ohlott, and Morrow (1994), Wick (1989).

Chapter 1: Linking Business Strategy and Experiences

1 A full discussion of strategy is beyond the scope of this book. Interested readers are directed to classic works on the topic such as Porter (1985), Miles and Snow (1978), and more recent approaches like Jim Collins's (2001) "hedgehog principle," figuring out what your organization can do better than anyone else.
2 See McCall, Lombardo, and Morrison (1988), Yost, Mannion-Plunkett, McKenna, and Homer (2001). For additional experiences see also Byham, Smith, and Paese (2002) and Lombardo and Eichinger (1988).
3 See Charan, Drotter, and Noel (2001) for a list of key transitions in the development of senior leaders.

Chapter 2: Linking Business Strategy and Competencies

1 See Yukl (2005), Judge, Colbert, and Ilies (2004), Judge, Bono, Ilies, and Gerhardt (2002).
2 See Arvey, Rotundo, Johnson, Zhang, and McGue (2006).
3 See Hollenbeck, McCall, and Silzer (2006), Zaccaro (2007).
4 Discussions of the impact of stretch assignments and cognitive ability on long-term leadership development can be seen in the AT&T longitudinal

leadership study (Howard & Bray, 1988) and discussed by Jacques (1986). See Sternberg (1988) for a broader theoretical discussion about the development of intelligence. See Roberts, Walton, and Viechtbauer (2006) for a discussion of personality changes over time.

5 See the uniform guidelines on employee selection procedures (Equal Employment Opportunity Commission, 1978) and *Principles for the Validation and Use of Personnel Selection Procedures* (Society for I-O Psychology, 2003).

6 McCall, Lombardo, and Morrison (1988).

Chapter 3: Linking Business Strategy and Relationships

1 See, for example, Balkundi and Kilduff (2006).
2 See Mintzberg (1983).
3 See McCauley and Douglas (2004).
4 See Birdi, Allan, and Warr (1997), McCall, Lombardo, and Morrison (1988), Noe (1996).
5 See Tharenou (1997).
6 See McCall et al. (1988).

Chapter 4: Talent Management Metrics to Watch

1 For additional measures, see the Corporate Leadership Council (2005).
2 See Becker, Huselid, and Ulrich (2001), Ittner and Larcker (2003).
3 Microsoft is currently conducting analyses of this type (Yost, 2006). See Mumford, Campion, and Morgeson (2007) for another example of this type of analysis.
4 See Jawahar and Williams (1997).

Chapter 5: Stepping into the Unknown

1 Clark and Lyness (1991) as cited in Ohlott (2004).
2 Appreciative Inquiry, a type of organizational development invention, suggests that the same mechanism occurs at the organizational level. Problems are important, but the most energy for improvement is created when they are discussed in the context of possibility (see Watkins & Mohr, 2001).
3 See McCall and Lombardo (1983).
4 Buckingham and Clifton (2001) have made this point elsewhere.
5 See McKenna and Yost (2004).

6 See Dweck (1986) for a comprehensive discussion of this idea.
7 See Heifitz and Linsky (2002), McKenna and Yost (2004).

Chapter 6: Stretch Assignments

1 See McCauley, Ruderman, Ohlott, and Morrow (1994). In our own work (Yost, Mannion-Plunkett, McKenna, & Homer, 2001), we found several of the same factors in addition to a number of support factors that also appeared to be critical.
2 See McCauley, Ohlott, and Ruderman (1999).

Chapter 7: Navigating the Experiences

1 See Yost and Plunkett (in press), Kanfer and Gaelick-Buys (1991).
2 See Bandura (2001), Manz (1986).
3 See Locke and Latham (1990).
4 See Gollwitzer (1999).
5 See McCall (1998), McCauley, Moxley, and Van Velsor (2004), and Yukl (2005) for broader discussions of organizational factors that are important in the creation of a development-focused organization.

Chapter 8: Real Time Reflection

1 See Seibert (1999).
2 See Argyris (1991).
3 See Baird, Holland, and Deacon (1999) and Ellis, Mendel, and Nir (2006) for more comprehensive descriptions of after-action reviews and the conditions necessary for their success.
4 See Baird et al. (1999), Ellis et al. (2006).

Chapter 9: When Leaders Derail

1 See McCall, Lombardo, and Morrison (1988).
2 See McCall and Lombardo (1983).
3 See Van Velsor and Leslie (1995), Hogan and Hogan (2001).
4 See McCall and Lombardo (1983).
5 See Hackman (2002) and Katzenbach and Smith (1997) among others.
6 See Van Velsor and Leslie (1995), Hogan and Hogan (2001).
7 See McClelland and Burnham (1976).
8 See McCall and Lombardo (1983).
9 See Buckingham and Clifton (2001) for strategies you can use to manage around your weaknesses.

Part III: Drawing on Other People

1 See Arthur and Rousseau (1996).
2 See Hall (1996).

Chapter 10: Development Conversations

1 See Kidd, Hirsh, and Jackson (2004).
2 Kidd et al. (2004).
3 See, for example, Noe (1996), Tracey, Tannenbaum, and Kavenagh (1995).
4 See Rosenthal and Rubin (1978).
5 See Eden (1992).
6 Eden (1992).
7 See Ashford and Black (1996).
8 See Heslin, VanderWalle, and Latham (2006).
9 See London (1997).
10 See Kluger and DeNisi (1996).
11 For thorough discussions of feedback and performance, see Cannon and Witherspoon (2005), Kluger and DeNisi (1996), London (1997).
12 See Kluger and DeNisi (1996).

Chapter 11: Role-Models

1 See Bandura (1986).
2 See Taylor, Russ-Eft, and Chan (2005).
3 See Ibarra (2004).
4 The research by the Center for Creative Leadership found that almost all role models were former bosses (McCall, Lombardo, & Morrison, 1988). Likewise Weaver, Treviño, and Agle (2005) found that ethical role models were never distant, but always someone the person had worked with closely.
5 See McCall et al. (1988). In our own research, we found that learning from role models was the experience named most often (Yost, Mannion-Plunkett, McKenna, & Homer, 2001). And as with the original research, one-third of the time these were bad leaders who served as living examples of what *not* to do.
6 See Bandura (1986).

Chapter 12: Mentoring

1 See Tharenou (1997).
2 See Higgins and Kram (2001), Ibarra (2000, 2004).

3 See Collins (1996).
4 See, for example, Eby, Durley, and Evans (2006).
5 See Allen, Poteet, Russell, and Dobbins (1997).
6 See Chao, Walz, and Gardner (1992), Ragins and Cotton (1999).

Chapter 13: Building Your Network

1 See Ibarra and Hunter (2007).
2 See also Higgins and Kram (2001).
3 See also Balkundi and Kilduff (2006).
4 See Cross and Parker (2004), Uzzi and Dunlap (2005).

Chapter 14: Individual Development Plans

1 Howard and Bray (1988) report that desire to be an executive was a very strong predictor of advancement correlating .62 with management level 20 years later. In the same study, cognitive ability correlated .38.
2 See Locke and Latham (1990).
3 See Garofano and Salas (2005).
4 These percentages are based on McCall, Lombardo, and Morrison (1988). Twenty years later, we found exactly the same percentages among leaders at Boeing (see Yost, Mannion-Plunkett, McKenna and Homer, 2001).
5 See the discussion in chapter 10.

Chapter 15: Performance Management

1 See Aguinis (2008).
2 See Shaw (2004) for a discussion of how the performance goal-setting process was enhanced at Microsoft to increase its effectiveness.
3 See Kerr (1995).
4 See DeNisi and Kluger (2000), Morgeson, Mumford, and Campion (2005).
5 See Colquitt, Conlon, Wesson, Porter, and Ng (2001), Gilliland and Langdon (1998).
6 See for example, Malos (1998) and Aguinis (2008).
7 See Aguinis (2008) for a full discussion of how performance management systems can be designed to minimize these biases and maximize their effectiveness.

Chapter 16: High Potential Programs

1 See discussion on the predictors of leadership emergence and effectiveness in chapter 2.

2 See Conger and Fulmer (2003).
3 See Karaevli and Hall (2003).
4 See Mintzberg (2004).
5 See also Byham, Smith, and Paese (2002).

Chapter 17: Succession Management

1 See Population Reference Bureau (2007).
2 Population Reference Bureau (2007).
3 See Karaevli and Hall (2003).
4 See Le Breton-Miller, Miller, and Steier (2004).
5 See Bower (2007), Conger and Fulmer (2003), Karaevli and Hall (2003).
6 See Byham, Smith, and Paese (2002).
7 See Boudreau and Ramstad (2007), Gerstein and Reisman (1983).

Chapter 18: Leadership Training Programs

1 See Burke and Day (1986), Collins and Holton (2004).
2 See Dotlich and Noel (1998), Marquardt (2004).
3 See Noe (1996), Tracey, Tannenbaum, and Kavenagh (1995)
4 See, for example, Gagne, Wager, Keller, and Golas (2004), Noe (2006).
5 See Knowles (1990).
6 See Marx (1982).

Chapter 19: Transitions

1 See Vaill (1989).
2 See Hall (1996).
3 See Dotlich, Noel, and Walker (2004).
4 See Charan, Drotter, and Noel (2001).
5 See Hill (1992), McCall, Lombardo, and Morrison (1988).
6 These strategies and others can be found in Bradt, Check, and Pedraza (2006) and Watkins (2003). Both books provide practical advice, tools, and checklists to manage transitions successfully.
7 See Watkins (2003).
8 See Gatewood, Feild, and Barrick (2008) for a thorough discussion of selection systems.

Chapter 20: Your Leadership Principles

1 See McKenna and Yost (2004).
2 See Den Hartog, House, Hanges, Ruiz-Quintanilla, and Dorfman (1999).
3 Weaver, Treviño, and Agle (2005) report the characteristics of people who were strong ethical role models.
4 See Wademan (2005).
5 See Fry (2003) for a discussion of the spiritual dimensions of leadership.
6 See Weaver et al. (2005).
7 See Treviño, Weaver, and Reynolds (2006).

Chapter 21: Your Legacy

1 See Zander and Zander (2000).
2 See, for example, Porter (1979).
3 See, for example, Schein (2004), Senge (1990).
4 See, for example, Kegan (1982), Levinson, Darrow, Klein, Levinson, and McKee (1978), Levinson and Levinson (1996).
5 See Kegan (1982), McCauley, Drath, Palus, O'Connor, and Baker (2006).
6 See Kegan (1994).
7 See Torbert (2004).
8 See Weick (1984).
9 See Friedman and Greenhaus (2000), Kossek and Lambert (2005).
10 See Ecclesiastes 1:2, King James Version and 2:18–19, New International Version.
11 See Hall and Chandler (2005), Wrzesniewski, McCauley, Rozin, and Schwartz (1997).
12 See Buechner (1993, p. 119).
13 See Collins (2001, pp. 96–7) for a discussion of how to identify your personal hedgehog principle.

References

Aguinis, H. (2008). *Performance management*, 2nd edn. Upper Saddle River, NJ: Pearson-Prentice Hall.

Allen, T. D., Poteet, M. L., Russell, J. E., & Dobbins, G. H. (1997). A field study of factors related to supervisors' willingness to mentor others. *Journal of Vocational Behavior*, **50**, 1–22.

Argyris, C. (1991). Teaching smart people how to learn. *Harvard Business Review*, **69(3)**, 99–109.

Arthur, M. B., & Rousseau, D. M. (1996). *The boundaryless career. A new employment principle for a new organizational era*. New York: Oxford University Press.

Arvey, R. D., Rotundo, M., Johnson, W., Zhang, Z., & McGue, M. (2006). The determinants of leadership role occupancy: Genetic and personality factors. *The Leadership Quarterly*, **17**, 1–20.

Ashford, S. J., & Black. J. S. (1996). Proactivity during organizational entry: The role of desire for control. *Journal of Applied Psychology*, **81**, 199–214.

Baird, L., Holland, P., & Deacon, S. (1999). Learning from action: Imbedding more learning into the performance fast enough to make a difference. *Organizational Dynamics*, **27(4)**, 19–32.

Balkundi, P., & Kilduff, M. (2006). The ties that lead: A social network approach to leadership. *Leadership Quarterly*, **17**, 419–39.

Bandura, A. (1986). *Social foundations of thought and action: A social cognitive theory*. Englewood Cliffs, NJ: Prentice-Hall.

Bandura, A. (2001). Social cognitive theory: An agentic perspective. *Annual Review of Psychology*, **52**, 1–26.

Becker, B. E., Huselid, M. A., & Ulrich, D. (2001). *The HR scorecard: Linking people, strategy, and performance*. Boston, MA: Harvard Business School Press.

Birdi, K., Allan, C., & Warr, P. (1997). Correlates and perceived outcomes of four types of employee development activity. *Journal of Applied Psychology*, **82**, 845–57.

Boudreau, J. W., & Ramstad, P. (2007). *Beyond HR: The new science of human capital.* Boston, MA: Harvard Business School Press.

Bower, J. L. (2007). Solve the succession crisis by growing inside-outside leaders. *Harvard Business Review*, **85**(11), 91–6.

Bradt, G., Check, J., & Pedraza, J. (2006). *The new leader's 100 day action plan: How to take charge, build your team, and get immediate results.* Hoboken, NJ: John Wiley & Sons.

Buckingham, M., & Clifton, D. O. (2001). *Now, discover your strengths.* New York: The Free Press.

Buechner, F. (1993). *Wishful thinking: A theological ABC.* New York: Harper Collins.

Burke, M. J., & Day, R. R. (1986). A cumulative study of the effectiveness of managerial training. *Journal of Applied Psychology*, **71**, 232–45.

Byham, W. C., Smith, A. B., & Paese, M. J. (2002). *Grow your own leaders: How to identify, develop, and retain leadership talent.* Upper Saddle River, NJ: Development Dimensions International Inc. & Prentice-Hall.

Cannon, M. D., & Witherspoon, R. (2005). Actionable feedback: Unlocking the power of learning and performance improvement. *Academy of Management Executive*, **19**, 120–34.

Chao G. T., Walz, P. M., & Gardner, P. D. (1992). Formal and informal mentorships: A comparison on mentoring functions and contrast with nonmentored counterparts. *Personnel Psychology*, **45**, 619–36.

Charan, R., Drotter, S., & Noel, J. (2001). *The leadership pipeline: How to build the leadership-powered company.* San Francisco: John Wiley.

Clark, L. A., & Lyness, K. S. (1991). Succession planning as a strategic activity at Citicorp. In L. W. Foster (ed.), *Advances in applied business strategy* (vol. 2, pp. 205–24). Greenwich, CT: JAI Press.

Collins, D. B., & Holton, E. F. (2004). The effectiveness of managerial leadership development programs: A meta-analysis of studies from 1982 to 2001. *Human Resource Development Quarterly*, **15**, 217–48.

Collins, J. (1996). Looking out for number one. *Inc.*, **18**(8), 29–30.

Collins, J. C. (2001). *Good to great.* New York: Harper Collins.

Colquitt, J. A., Conlon, D. E., Wesson, M. J., Porter, C. O., & Ng, K. Y. (2001). Justice at the millennium: A meta-analysis of 25 years of organizational justice research. *Journal of Applied Psychology*, **86**, 425–45.

Conger, J. A., & Fulmer, R. M. (2003). Developing your leadership pipeline. *Harvard Business Review*, **81**(12), 76–84.

Corporate Leadership Council. (2005). *The metrics standard: Establishing standards for 200 core human capital measures.* Washington, DC: Corporate Executive Board.

Cross, R., & Parker, A. (2004). *The hidden power of social networks.* Boston, MA: Harvard Business School Press.

Den Hartog, D. N., House, R. J., Hanges, P. J., Ruiz-Quintanilla, S. A., & Dorfman, P. W. (1999). Culture specific and cross-culturally generalizable implicit leadership theories: Are attributes of charismatic/ transformational leadership universally endorsed? *Leadership Quarterly,* **10,** 219–56.

DeNisi, A. S., & Kluger, A. N. (2000). Feedback effectiveness: Can 360-degree appraisals be improved? *Academy of Management Executive,* **14,** 129–39.

Dotlich, D. L., & Noel, J. L. (1998). *Action learning: How the world's top companies are recreating their leaders and themselves.* San Francisco, CA: Jossey-Bass.

Dotlich, D. L., Noel, J. L., & Walker, N. (2004). *Leadership passages: The personal and professional transitions that make or break a leader.* San Francisco, CA: Jossey-Bass.

Dweck, C. S. (1986). Motivational processes affecting learning, *American Psychologist,* **41,** 1040–8.

Eby, L. T., Durley, J. R., & Evans, S. C. (2006). The relationship between short-term mentoring benefits and long-term mentor outcomes. *Journal of Vocational Behavior,* **69,** 424–44.

Eden, D. (1992). Leadership and expectations: Pygmalion effects and other self-fulfilling prophesies in organizations. *Leadership Quarterly,* **3,** 271–305.

Ellis, S., Mendel, R. & Nir, M. (2006). Learning from successful and failed experience: The moderating role of kind of after-event review. *Journal of Applied Psychology,* **91,** 669–80.

Equal Employment Opportunity Commission, Civil Service Commission, Department of Labor & Department of Justice. (1978). Adoption by four agencies of uniform guidelines on employee selection procedures. *Federal Register,* **43,** 38290–315.

Friedman, S. D., & Greenhaus, J. H. (2000). *Work and family – allies or enemies? What happens when business professionals confront life choices.* New York: Oxford University Press.

Fry, L. W. (2003). Toward a theory of spiritual leadership. *Leadership Quarterly,* **14,** 693–727.

Gagne, R. M., Wager, W. W., Keller, J. M., & Golas, K. (2004). *Principles of instructional design,* 5th edn. Belmont, CA: Wadsworth.

Garofano, C. M., & Salas, E. (2005). What influences continuous employee development decisions? *Human Resource Management Review,* **15,** 281–304.

Gatewood, R., Feild, H., & Barrick, M. (2008). *Human resource selection.* Mason, OH: Thompson Higher Education.

Gerstein, M, & Reisman, H. (1983). Strategic selection: Matching executives to business conditions. *Sloan Management Review,* **24(2),** 33–49.

Gilliland, S. W., & Langdon, J. C. (1998). Creating performance management systems that promote perceptions of fairness. In J. W. Smither (ed.), *Performance appraisal: State of the art in practice* (pp. 49–94). San Francisco, CA: Jossey-Bass.

Gollwitzer, P. M. (1999). Implementation intentions and effective goal pursuit: Strong effects of simple plans. *American Psychologist*, **54**, 493–503.

Hackman, J. R. (2002). *Leading teams: Setting the stage for great performances.* Boston, MA: Harvard Business School Press.

Hall, D. T. (1996). *The career is dead – long live the career: A relational approach to careers.* San Francisco, CA, Jossey-Bass.

Hall, D. T., & Chandler, D. E. (2005). Psychological success: When the career is a calling. *Journal of Organizational Behavior*, **26**, 155–76.

Heifitz, R. A., & Linsky, M. (2002). A survival guide for leaders. *Harvard Business Review*, **80(6)**, 65–74.

Heslin, P. A., VandeWalle, D., & Latham, G. P. (2006). Keen to help? Managers' implicit person theories and their subsequent employee coaching. *Personnel Psychology*, **59**, 871–902.

Higgins, M. C., & Kram, K. E. (2001). Reconceptualizing mentoring at work: A developmental network perspective. *Academy of Management Review*, **26**, 264–88.

Hill, L. A. (1992). *Becoming a manager.* Boston, MA: Harvard Business School Press.

Hogan, R., & Hogan, J. (2001). Assessing leadership: A view from the dark side. *International Journal of Selection and Assessment*, **9**, 40–51.

Hollenbeck, G. P., McCall, M. W., & Silzer, R. F. (2006). Leadership competency models. *Leadership Quarterly*, **17**, 398–413.

Howard, A., & Bray, D. W. (1988). *Managerial lives in transition: Advancing age and changing times.* New York: Guilford Press.

Ibarra, H. (2000). Making partner: A mentor's guide to the psychological journey. *Harvard Business Review*, **78(2)**, 146–55.

Ibarra, H. (2004). *Working identity: Unconventional strategies for reinventing your career.* Cambridge, MA: Harvard Business School Press.

Ibarra, H., & Hunter, M. (2007). How leaders create and use networks. *Harvard Business Review*, **85(1)**, 40–7.

Ittner, C. D., & Larcker, D. F. (2003). Coming up short: On nonfinancial performance measurement. *Harvard Business Review*, **81(11)**, 88–95.

Jacques, E. (1986). The development of intellectual capability: A discussion of stratified systems theory. *Journal of Applied Behavioral Science*, **22**, 361–84.

Jawahar, I. M., & William, C. R. (1997). Where all the children are above average: The performance appraisal purpose effect. *Personnel Psychology*, **50**, 905–25.

Judge, T. A., Bono, J. E., Ilies, R., & Gerhardt, M. W. (2002). Personality and leadership: A qualitative and quantitative review. *Journal of Applied Psychology*, **87**, 765–80.

Judge, T. A., Colbert, A. E., & Ilies, R. (2004). Intelligence and leadership: A quantitative review and test of theoretical propositions. *Journal of Applied Psychology*, **81**, 542–52.

Kanfer, F. H., & Gaelick-Buys, L. (1991). Self-management methods. In F. H. Kanfer & A. P. Goldstein (eds), *Helping people change: A textbook of methods* (4th edn, pp. 305–60). New York: Pergamon Press.

Karaevli, A., & Hall, D. T. (2003). Growing leaders for turbulent times: Is succession planning up to the challenge? *Organizational Dynamics*, **32**, 62–79.

Katzenbach, J. R., & Smith, D. K. (1997). *The wisdom of teams: Creating the high-performance organization*. New York: HarperBusiness.

Kegan, R. (1982). *The evolving self: Problem and process in human development*. Cambridge, MA: Harvard University Press.

Kegan, R. (1994). *In over our heads: The mental demands of modern life*. Cambridge, MA: Harvard University Press.

Kerr, S. (1995). On the folly of rewarding A, while hoping for B. *Academy of Management Executive*, **9**, 7–14.

Kidd, J. M., Hirsh, W., & Jackson, C. (2004). Straight talking: The nature of effective career discussions at work. *Journal of Career Development*, **30**, 231–45.

Kluger, A., & DeNisi, A. (1996). The effects of feedback interventions on performance: A historical review, a meta-analysis, and a preliminary feedback intervention theory. *Psychological Bulletin*, **119**, 254–84.

Knowles, M. (1990). *The adult learner*, 4th edn. Houston, TX: Gulf Publishing.

Kossek, E. E., & Lambert, S. J. (2005). *Work and life integration: Organizational, cultural, and individual perspectives*. Mahwah, NJ: Lawrence Erlbaum.

Le Breton-Miller, I., Miller, D., & Steier, L. P. (2004). Toward an integrative model of effective FOB succession. *Entrepreneurial Theory and Practice*, **28**, 305–28.

Levinson, D. J., Darrow, C. N., Klein, E. B., Levinson, M. L., & McKee, B. (1978). *The seasons of a man's life*. New York: Knopf.

Levinson, D. J., & Levinson, J. D. (1996). *The seasons of a woman's life*. New York: Knopf.

Locke, E. A., & Latham, G. P. (1990). *A theory of goal setting and task performance*. Englewood Cliffs, NJ: Prentice Hall.

Lombardo, M. M., & Eichinger, R. W. (1988). *Eighty-eight assignments for development in place*. Greensboro, NC: Center for Creative Leadership.

London, M. (1997). *Job feedback: Giving, seeking, and using feedback for performance improvement.* Mahwah, NJ: Lawrence Erlbaum.

Malos, S. B. (1998). Current legal issues in performance appraisal. In J. W. Smither (ed.), *Performance appraisal: State of the art in practice* (pp. 49–94). San Francisco, CA: Jossey-Bass.

Manz, C. C. (1986.) Self-leadership: Toward an expanded theory of self-influence processes in organizations. *Academy of Management Review,* **11**, 585–600.

Marquardt, M. J. (2004). *Optimizing the power of action learning: Solving problems and building leaders in real time.* Palo Alto, CA: Consulting Psychologists Press, Inc.

Marx, R. D. (1982). Relapse prevention for managerial training: A model for maintenance of behavioral change. *Academy of Management Review,* **7**, 433–41.

McCall, M. W. (1998). *High flyers: Developing the next generation of leaders.* Boston, MA: Harvard Business School Press.

McCall, M. W., & Lombardo, M. M. (1983). *Off the track: Why and how successful executives get derailed (Tech. Rep. No. 21).* Greensboro, NC: Center for Creative Leadership.

McCall, M. W., Lombardo, M. M., & Morrison, A. M. (1988). *The lessons of experience: How successful executives develop on the job.* New York: The Free Press.

McCauley, C. D., & Douglas, C. A. (2004). Developmental relationships. In C. D. McCauley & E. Van Velsor (eds), *Handbook of leadership development* (2nd edn, pp. 85–115). Greensboro, NC: Center for Creative Leadership.

McCauley, C. D., Drath, W. H., Palus, C. J., O'Connor, P. M. G., & Baker, B. A. (2006). The use of constructive-developmental theory to advance the understanding of leadership. *Leadership Quarterly,* **17**, 634–53.

McCauley, C. D., Moxley, R. S., & Van Velsor, E. (2004). *The Center for Creative Leadership handbook of leadership development.* San Francisco, CA: Jossey-Bass.

McCauley, C. D., Ohlott, P. J., & Ruderman, M. N. (1999). *Job challenge profile: Facilitator's guide and participant's workbook.* Greensboro, NC: Center for Creative Leadership.

McCauley, C. D., Ruderman, M. N., Ohlott, P. J., & Morrow, J. E. (1994). Assessing the developmental components of managerial jobs. *Journal of Applied Psychology,* **79**, 544–60.

McClelland, D. C., & Burnham, D. H. (1976). Power is the great motivator. *Harvard Business Review,* **54(2)**, 100–10.

McKenna, R. B., & Yost, P. R. (2004). The differentiated leader: Specific strategies for handling today's adverse situations. *Organizational Dynamics,* **33**, 292–306.

Miles, R. E., & Snow, C. C. (1978). *Organizational strategy, structure, and process.* New York: McGraw-Hill.

Mintzberg, H. (1983). *Power in and around organizations.* Englewood Cliffs, NJ: Prentice Hall.

Mintzberg, H. (2004). *Managers not MBAs: A hard look at the soft practice of managing and management development.* San Francisco, CA: Berrett-Koehler.

Morgeson, F. P., Mumford, T. V., & Campion, M. A. (2005). Coming full circle: Using research and practice to address 27 questions about 360-degree feedback programs. *Consulting Psychology Journal: Practice and Research,* **57**, 196–209.

Mumford, T. V., Campion, M. A., & Morgeson, F. P. (2007). The leadership skills strataplex: Leadership skill requirements across organizational levels. *Leadership Quarterly,* **18**, 154–66.

Noe, R. A. (1996). Is career management related to employee development and performance? *Journal of Organizational Behavior,* **17**, 119–33.

Noe, R. A. (2006). *Employee training and development,* 4th edn. Boston, MA: McGraw-Hill.

Ohlott, P. J. (2004). Job assignments. In C. D. McCauley & E. Van Velsor (eds), *Handbook of leadership development* (2nd edn, pp. 151–82), Greensboro, NC: Center for Creative Leadership.

Population Reference Bureau. (2007). 2007 World Population Data Sheet, 1–16. Retrieved May 20, 2008, from http://www.prb.org/Publications/Datasheets/2007/2007WorldPopulationDataSheet.aspx.

Porter, M. E. (1979, Mar/Apr). How competitive forces shape strategy, *Harvard Business Review,* **57**(2), 137–45.

Porter, M. E. (1985). *Competitive advantage: Creating and sustaining superior performance.* New York: The Free Press.

Ragins B. R., & Cotton, J. L. (1999). Mentor functions and outcomes: A comparison of men and women in formal and informal mentoring relationships. *Journal of Applied Psychology,* **84**, 529–50.

Roberts, B. W., Walton, K. E., & Viechtbauer, W. (2006). Patterns of mean-level change in personality traits across the life course: A meta-analysis of longitudinal studies. *Psychological Bulletin,* **132**, 1–25.

Rosenthal, R., & Rubin, D. B. (1978). Interpersonal expectancy effects: The first 345 studies. *Behavioral and Brain Sciences,* **3**, 377–86.

Schein, E. H. (2004). *Organizational culture and leadership,* 3rd edn. San Francisco, CA: Jossey-Bass.

Seibert, K. W. (1999). Reflection-in-action: Tools for cultivating on-the-job learning conditions. *Organizational Dynamics,* **27**(3), 54–65.

Senge, P. M. (1990). The leader's new work: Building learning organizations. *Sloan Management Review,* **32**(1), 7–23.

Shaw, K. N. (2004). Changing the goal-setting process at Microsoft. *Academy of Management Executive*, **18**, 139–42.

Society for Industrial/Organizational Psychology (2003). *Principles for the validation and use of personnel selection procedures*, 4th edn. Bowling Green, OH: SIOP.

Sternberg, R. J. (1988). Applying cognitive theory to the testing and teaching of intelligence. *Applied Cognitive Psychology*, **2**, 231–55.

Taylor, P. J., Russ-Eft, D. F., & Chan, D. W. L. (2005). A meta-analytic review of behavior modeling training. *Journal of Applied Psychology*, **90**, 692–709.

Tharenou, P. (1997). Explanations of managerial career advancement. *Australian Psychologist*, **32**, 19–28.

Torbert, W. (2004). *Action inquiry: The secret of timely and transforming leadership*. San Francisco, CA: Berrett-Koehler.

Tracey, J. B., Tannenbaum, S. I., & Kavenagh, M. J. (1995). Applying trained skills on the job: The importance of work environment. *Journal of Applied Psychology*, **80**, 239–52.

Treviño, L. K., Weaver, G. R., & Reynolds, S. J. (2006). Behavioral ethics in organizations: A review. *Journal of Management*, **32**, 951–90.

Uzzi, B., & Dunlap, S. (2005). How to build your network. *Harvard Business Review*, **83(12)**, 53–60.

Vaill, P. (1989). *Managing as a performing art*. San Francisco, CA: Jossey-Bass.

Van Velsor, E., & Leslie, J. B. (1995). Why executives derail: Perspectives across time and cultures. *Academy of Management Executive*, **9(4)**, 62–72.

Wademan, D. (2005). The best advice I ever got. *Harvard Business Review*, **83(1)**, 35–44.

Watkins, J. M., & Mohr, B. J. (2001). *Appreciative inquiry: Change at the speed of imagination*. San Francisco: Jossey-Bass/Pfeiffer.

Watkins, M. (2003). *The first 90 days: Critical success strategies for new leaders at all levels*. Boston, MA: Harvard Business School Press.

Weaver, G. R., Treviño, L. K., & Agle, B. (2005). "Somebody I look up to": Ethical role models in organizations. *Organizational Dynamics*, **34**, 313–30.

Weick, K. E. (1984). Small wins: Redefining the scale of social problems. *American Psychologist*, **39**, 40–9.

Wick, C. W. (1989). How people develop. An in-depth look. *HR Reporter*, **6(7)**, 1–3.

Wrzesniewski, A., McCauley, C. R., Rozin, P., & Schwartz, B. (1997). Jobs, careers, and callings: People's relations to their work. *Journal of Research in Personality*, **31**, 21–33.

Yost, P. R. (2006). *State of the art in talent management: Developmental assignments.* Invited address conducted at the Leading Edge Consortium, The Society for Industrial/Organizational Psychology, Charlotte, NC, October 27–8.

Yost, P. R., Mannion-Plunkett, M., McKenna, R. B., & Homer, L. (2001). Lessons of experience: Personal and situational factors that drive growth. In R. B. McKenna (Chair), *Leadership development: The strategic use of on-the-job assignments.* Symposium conducted at the Society for Industrial/ Organizational Psychology, San Diego, CA, April 27–29.

Yost, P. R., & Plunkett, M. M. (in press). Developing leadership talent through experiences. In R. Silzer, & B. Dowell (eds.), *Strategy driven talent management: A leadership imperative.* San Francisco, CA: Jossey-Bass.

Yukl, G. (2005). *Leadership in organizations,* 6th edn. Upper Saddle River, NJ: Prentice-Hall.

Zaccaro, S. J. (2007). Trait-based perspectives on leadership. *American Psychologist,* **62**, 6–16.

Zander, R. S., & Zander, B. (2000). *The art of possibility: Transforming personal and professional life.* Boston, MA: Harvard Business School Press.

Index

learning
  career derailment and, 79, 80
  culture of, 206–7
  development conversations, 91,
    95
  focus on, 49–50, 52–3, 204
  from experiences, 63–70,
    71–6
  from role models, 101–7
  high potential programs, 147
  leadership training programs,
    165, 168, 174–5
legacies, 179, 195–202
life roles, 201–2
life–work structure, 198, 204–5
luck, 86

measuring leadership development
    see metrics
mentors, 25, 50, 109–16, 204
metrics, 33–41
  start-up experiences, 9, 10
  stretch organizations, 60
Mintzberg, Henry, 25, 149
motivation strategies, 64–6, 67–9
  see also real-time reflection

networks, 21, 25, 110
  building, 117–25
  effectiveness assessment,
    124–5
  failure to build, 85
  leadership training programs,
    174
  legacies, 200
  stretch assignments, 50, 52, 56,
    59
  for team's development,
    205–6
  types of, 118
  see also support systems
Noel, James, 182

observational learning, 101–2
operational networks, 118
organizational culture see culture,
    organizational
organizational leadership bench
    strength, 33, 34–5, 36, 37,
    39, 41
organizational needs analyses, 166–
    7, 170–1
organizational review meetings,
    161–2
organizational talent management,
    33, 35–6
outcome talent management
    metrics, 37

performance
  career derailment, 83
  development conversations, 91,
    92–3, 95–6
  focus on, 203
  high potential programs, 149–50
performance culture, 205
performance goals, 133, 134–5, 139,
    140–1, 146, 206
performance management, 35, 39,
    42, 82, 139–46, 206
performance orientation, 49, 50,
    52–3
personal networks, 118
potential
  focus on, 48, 51, 52
  high potential programs, 145,
    147–54
  identifying high, 149, 150
primacy effect, 145
principle-based organizations, 193,
    207
priorities, evaluating, 81, 201, 204
procedural justice, 143
process talent management metrics,
    37